METTLE

MENTAL TOUGHNESS TRAINING FOR LAW ENFORCEMENT

Laurence Miller, PhD

Looseleaf
Law Publications, Inc.

43-08 162nd Street • Flushing, NY 11358
www.LooseleafLaw.com • 800-647-5547

First printing, 2008   Fourth printing, 2012
Second printing, 2009   Fifth printing, 2018
Third printing, 2010
ISBN: 978-1-932777-62-8

Library of Congress Cataloging-in-Publication Data

Miller, Laurence, 1951-
   M.E.T.T.L.E. : mental toughness training for law enforcement / Laurence Miller.
      p. cm.
   ISBN 978-1-932777-62-8
 1. Police training. 2. Law enforcement--Psychological aspects. 3. Mental discipline. 4. Police psychology. I. Title. II. Title: METTLE. III. Title: Mental-toughness training for law enforcement.
   HV7923.M55 2007
   363.2'2--dc22   2007026561

Cover design by Sans Serif Inc., Saline, Michigan

CONTENTS

INTRODUCTION

Psychology and Law Enforcement in the Real Damn World

> **Mettle:** Character or temperament; courage; pluck; aroused to one's best efforts; full of spirit; courageous; valiant.
>
> —*Funk and Wagnall's Standard Dictionary*

When I was in high school, a friend and I decided it was time we toughened up, so we pooled our change and bought a book called *Teach Yourself Karate.* This slim drugstore paperback was filled with grainy black-and-white photos of high-kicking men on low-lying mats, supplemented by a thin instructional text in barely comprehensible English. I was skeptical: can you really learn a complex martial arts technique by reading a book? But my friend was determined and we spent many hours emulating and practicing the kicks, chops, thrusts, and blocks we saw on those pages. After a while, it seemed like we'd gotten down the fundamentals (as long as, I secretly suspected, we didn't actually have to *fight* anybody). But eventually I lost interest and let him have the book.

My friend didn't give up, though. He went on to take real-life karate training at a local dojo, ultimately earned a black belt and became a karate instructor himself. Years later, when I discussed the episode with him, he told me that he really learned only the rudimentary basics of karate from reading the book, but I still remember his words about that little instruction manual: "It gave me the foundation, the knowledge, something I could build on. I had to do the hard work, but that book gave me the *oomph*."

So it is that I'm often asked if something as critical and complex as mental toughness training can really be learned from a book or course. It's the same question that applies to every other area I teach and train: crisis intervention, police psychology, forensic behavioral science, business management, psychotherapy, neuropsychology. It's the same, in fact, with virtually every complex field of human endeavor: medicine, law enforcement, firefighting, military training, airline piloting, sports, music—you can add your own items to this list. But the honest answer is always the same: The books and the courses by themselves won't make you an expert.

But what they can do is give you the foundation, the background knowledge, the accumulated wisdom behind your profession or discipline; otherwise, why do you think doctors go to medical school, managers get MBAs, and you attended the police academy? In the education and training phases, you learn the basics, you build the foundation. Then, going on to practice and train in simulations and real-life settings gives you the expertise to be a true professional; your motivation to excel will give you the *oomph.* But you have to start somewhere. If this weren't true, there'd be no need for books, courses, or training materials in any field. My friend got his black belt, but he started with a black-and-white paperback.

But of course, we need the *right* training materials. Because law enforcement professionals have traditionally viewed psychology and the behavioral sciences with mistrust, a number of authors have well-meaningly attempted to bridge these domains by showing how psychology can be practically applied to the challenges of police work. Most of these professionals are primarily law enforcement personnel who try to select areas of psychology that they then apply to their respective domains. We've seen this most prominently in the field of investigative behavioral science and criminal profiling and in the area of stress management. Only recently have psychologists themselves begun to apply psychology to the daily challenges of policing and especially to handling the sometimes life-and-death scenarios that characterize police work.

For example, how do you keep your adrenalin under control during an armed standoff or hostage situation? How do you counteract tunnel vision in the midst of an officer-involved-shooting scenario? During a potentially dangerous building search or traffic stop, how do you keep your attention focused on the immediate hazards, while scanning the environment for additional threats? What if you're cold-cocked from behind? How do you ensure that a deadly struggle with a murderous suspect ends up with you going home that night? How do you develop the resilience to bounce back from a traumatic critical incident with minimal scars on your psyche?

METTLE: Mental Toughness Training for Law Enforcement grew out of my experiences as a police psychologist teaching and training officers in the somewhat amorphous field of "stress management." What quickly became apparent is that the kinds of stresses experienced by police officers don't lend themselves very well to the kinds of fuzzy-wuzzy techniques that are often taught in traditional stress management courses and books. As an officer, you live in the real damn world. You need to know how to use your brain as a tool to survive and prevail in a critical encounter, not sit around and sing, "Kumbaya." Until now, there has really been no comprehensive stress-management guide of this type for law enforcement.

But I'm not reinventing the wheel. There already exists a vast literature from the fields of military psychology, sports psychology, cognitive psychology, neuropsychology, and behavioral medicine that is directly applicable to a mental toughness curriculum for law enforcement. If you flip to the back of this book and find yourself choking on the bibliography, there's a reason for that: You have now entered a no-bullshit zone. Every principle and technique described in this book is based on well-validated, scientific principles of psychology, behavioral science, and law enforcement. I respect my readers' intelligence by letting them see exactly where my ideas and methods come from and how I've synthesized and enhanced them to develop the METTLE model. You can totally ignore the references and still get maximal benefit from this volume. But I hope you'll want to learn more, to go further than these pages, to adapt and expand the techniques in this book to your own law enforcement domain—patrol, undercover, SWAT, hostage negotiation, drug interdiction, criminal investigation, and so on. That's the ITTS principle you'll learn in Chapter 2.

Look, I want you to buy this book, but I'm not going to promise what I can't deliver, what no book can deliver. Just passively reading these pages won't turn you into a Supercop, just as reading a book or sitting in a class on firearms, communications, or martial arts won't automatically make you an exponent of those skills. You have to do the work, practice the mental kicks, chops, and blocks, try out the strategies, be willing to accept honest feedback about your efforts, fine-tune your moves, and try again.

But just because something takes effort doesn't mean it has to be boring or painful. Keep at it and an amazing thing will happen: You'll find yourself managing daily stresses better and dealing with critical emergencies like a mental ninja. You'll learn that *mental toughness* means flexibility, resilience, and decisiveness of action. You'll gradually weave your skills together to develop your unique and individualized *psychological body armor*. And with continued practice and willingness to learn, you'll progress from tentative novice, to adept practitioner, and finally to the sublime confidence of a true master.

If you are an officer, think of this book as a user-friendly law enforcement psychology training manual, a practical guide to the essential psychophysiological skills you'll need to handle daily stresses on the job and deal decisively and successfully with critical emergencies, a head start and a head's-up toward getting and keeping your *oomph.*

And if you're a mental health clinician who consults with law enforcement, use this manual as a clinical and training tool to maximize your effectiveness at every stage of your educational interaction and therapeutic intervention with the men and women who risk their lives to keep us safe.

METTLE: Mental Toughness Training for Law Enforcement is organized into four parts. The two chapters in Part I introduce the basic principles of stress management and crisis intervention for law enforcement and describe the basic components of the METTLE model. While it is not essential to assimilate all of the theory behind the techniques to follow, I recommend you at least survey the contents, so you'll have an idea of where the building blocks of the METTLE model come from and how they fit into an overall philosophy and technology of law enforcement psychological training.

Part II provides a blow-by-blow description of the particular strategies and techniques utilized in my courses and training seminars, as well as the scientific principles that underlie them. These are the mental skills that proactively build your psychological body armor and that will prepare you to handle both ordinary stresses and life-and-death emergencies on the job. These chapters should be read in sequence as the techniques therein are intended to be used in an organic, interactive way in real-life critical situations. But as I said earlier, just reading them won't make you proficient—as in anything worth doing, the three magic words of mastery are: *practice, practice,* and *practice.*

In Part III you learn what to do after a life-threatening critical incident has occurred. The techniques described in these chapters are adaptations of law enforcement group and individual debriefing and counseling methods that are specifically applied to the task of reinforcing the officer's resilience and ability to bounce back from a critical incident. This is the section of the book that should be carefully read by mental health clinicians who consult with police agencies because the practical, down-to-earth psychological treatment strategies discussed may not be familiar to the typical psychotherapist or counselor.

As I noted above, hopefully, one of the most important things this book will do for you is enable you to adapt the METTLE model to your own particular domain of law enforcement. Part IV gives you a head start in describing some particular applications of METTLE to two common but important areas of police work: suspect and vehicle searches on patrol and officer-involved shootings. If you can master the METTLE model and techniques in these vital areas, you can apply them to any domain of police work you choose to work in.

I write this book with gratitude and appreciation for the work of all law enforcement men and women everywhere and with the personal admiration for many of the cops and agents I have come to work with closely and know well. I hope this volume will make your jobs safer and more effective, and I welcome any and all feedback from my readers—as noted in Chapter 2, ITTS also applies to yours truly. Stay safe.

ABOUT THE AUTHOR

Laurence Miller, PhD, is a clinical and forensic psychologist, educator and trainer, author and speaker, and law enforcement consultant based in Boca Raton, Florida. Dr. Miller is the police psychologist for the West Palm Beach Police Department, mental health advisor for Troop L of the Florida Highway Patrol, a forensic psychological examiner for the Palm Beach County Court, an expert witness in civil and criminal cases, and a consulting psychologist with several regional and national law enforcement and public safety agencies and private corporations. Dr. Miller is a certified trainer by the International Critical Incident Stress Foundation (ICISF) and is a member of the Psychology Services Section of the International Association of Chiefs of Police (IACP), the International Law Enforcement Educators and Trainers Association (ILEETA), and the Society for Police and Criminal Psychology (SPCP).

Dr. Miller is an instructor at the Criminal Justice Institute of Palm Beach Community College and at Florida Atlantic University. He conducts continuing educational programs and training seminars around the country, appears on radio and TV, and is the author of over 200 professional and popular print and on-line publications pertaining to the brain, behavior, health, law enforcement, police psychology, criminal justice, and organizational management. He maintains an interactive police psychology column on the PoliceOne website (www.policeone.com). His previous books include *Shocks to the System: Psychotherapy of Traumatic Disability Syndromes* (W.W. Norton) and *Practical Police Psychology: Stress Management and Crisis Intervention for Law Enforcement* (Charles C. Thomas). Dr. Miller can be contacted at (561) 392-8881 or on-line at docmilphd@aol.com.

PART I:

*Extreme Stress and Mental Toughness
in Law Enforcement*

1

Basic Principles of Stress Management and Crisis Intervention in Law Enforcement

The Stresses and Challenges of Policing: Developing Your *Psychological Body Armor*

The world of policing at the beginning of the 21st century is in some respects unique, in other ways linked to the past (Peak, 2003; Toch & Grant, 2005; Miller, 2006*l*; in press-f). The traditional role of the law enforcement officer has always been fighting crime, but today's urban, rural, local, and federal law enforcement agencies are confronted with a host of unique challenges, only some of which involve the actual apprehension of criminals. On any given day, these may include resolving a dispute between retail merchants; helping a homeless person get to a shelter; finding a lost child; settling a family or neighbor squabble; taking a mentally disturbed citizen into protective custody; dispersing an unruly crowd of teens; making several traffic stops; applying first aid to an accident victim; or referring an ill, indigent, or elderly person to social services.

All of these tasks require some combination of technical expertise and interpersonal skill, and most can be handled by some combination of mediation, arbitration, deft communication, and appropriate assertion of police authority (Miller, 2006*l*). But even seemingly innocuous encounters can turn deadly in a flash and any of these situations could devolve into a dangerous crisis situation if handled clumsily or ineffectively. And even when you do everything right, follow your training,

3

use all of your skills, the unpredictability of human nature virtually assures that some situations will escalate out of control. In many of these cases, officers often look back and report that, "I didn't see that one coming."

In fact, unlike the Hollywood portrayals, most officer injuries or fatalities don't occur in the context of pitched battles with gangsters or terrorists, but rather in the course of routine police activities, such as traffic stops, citizen disputes, or domestic calls. That's why mastery of the METTLE skills presented in this book can be thought of as a kind of *psychological body armor* that protects law enforcement officers from unnecessary physical and psychological risks as they carry out their sworn duties to protect and serve. One of the functions of this book is to guide officers in refining, expanding and solidifying the self-regulation and interpersonal skills that many of you already use intuitively to manage stress and crises on the job. This will serve the dual function of (1) making your police work more effective in the here-and-now; and (2) reducing your chances of developing stress and traumatic disability syndromes down the road.

Because most advances in the science and practice of any field are built on what has gone before, we begin with a little background.

History of Stress and Trauma in Psychology

Historically, the pendulum of interest in stress syndromes has swung back and forth between military and civilian traumas (Evans, 1992; Pizarro, 2006; Rosen, 1975; Trimble, 1981; Wilson, 1994). During warfare, rulers and generals have always had an interest in knowing as much as possible about factors that might adversely affect their fighting forces. To this end, doctors have been pressed into service to diagnose and treat soldiers with the aim of getting them back to the front lines as quickly as possible. In times of peace, attention turns to the everyday accidents and individual acts of violence that can produce stress, pain, and trauma in the lives of civilians.

The ancient Greeks and Romans wrote eloquently about the trials and travails that could afflict the warrior mind (Sherman, 2005). One of the first modern conceptualizations of post-traumatic stress was put forth by the army surgeon Hoffer who, in 1678, developed the concept of *nostalgia,* which he defined as a deterioration in the physical and mental health of homesick soldiers. The cause of this malady was attributed to the formation of abnormally vivid images in the affected soldier's brain by battle-induced over-excitation of the "vital spirits." Here, in effect, was one of the first attempts to explain how a psychological event could affect brain functioning and, in turn, influence health and behavior.

With the 18th and 19th centuries came the monstrous machines of the Industrial Revolution to crush, grind, and flay scores of hapless workers who toiled nearby. At about the same time, a new form of high-speed transportation, the railroad, began strewing many of its passengers about in derailments and collisions. All too often, after the physical scars had healed, or even when injury to the body was minor or nonexistent, many industrial or railway accident victims showed persisting disturbances in thought, feeling, and action that could not readily be explained by the conventional medical knowledge of the day.

In 1882, Erichson introduced the concept of *railway spine,* which he attributed to as-yet unobservable perturbations in the structure of the central nervous system caused by blows to the body. Other physicians of the time considered the strange disorders of sensation and movement to be due to disruptions in blood flow to the spinal cord, or even to unobservable small hemorrhages.

While these researchers focused on the physical, others began to view the origin of post-traumatic impairment syndromes as a psychological phenomenon, albeit straying none too far from the home base of neurophysiology. This was expressed in Page's (1895) theory of *nervous shock* which posited that a state of overwhelming fright or terror was the primary cause of traumatic impairment syndromes in railway and industrial accidents. Similarly, at around the same time, Oppenheim (1890) theorized that a strong enough stimulus perceived through the senses might jar the nervous system into a state of disequilibrium.

For his part, the great French physician Charcot (1887) regarded the effects of physical trauma as a form of *hysteria*, the symptoms arising as a consequence of disordered brain physiology caused by the terrifying memory of the traumatic event. In postulating the impact of a psychological force on the physical functioning of the brain, these late 19th century theories were reminiscent of Hoffer's conceptualization, two centuries earlier, except that electrophysiological impulses now had replaced vital spirits as the underlying mechanism of the disorder.

Attention, however, soon shifted back to the field of battle. The American Civil War introduced a new level of industrialized killing and, with it, a dramatic increase in reports of stress-related nervous ailments. Further advances in weapons technology during the First World War produced an alarming accumulation of horrific battlefield casualties from machine guns, poison gas, and long-range artillery. The latter led to the widely applied concept of *shell shock,* initially believed to be caused by the brain-concussive effects of exploding shells, but later understood to be a form of psychological incapacitation resulting from the trauma of battle.

To this end, physicians continued to marshal new findings about the role of the nervous system in regulating states of arousal and bodily homeostasis. Wilson and his colleagues (Frazier & Wilson, 1918; Mearburg & Wilson, 1918) described a syndrome in traumatized soldiers they called *irritable heart*, which they attributed to overstimulation of the sympathetic ("fight-or-flight") branch of the autonomic nervous system.

Even Sigmund Freud got into the act. No stranger to neuro-scientific theory and practice himself (Miller, 1991), Freud (1920) initially regarded the tendency to remain mentally fixated on traumatic events as having a biological basis. But recurring recollections and nightmares of a frightening nature seemed to fly in the face of Freud's theory of the pleasure principle. Consequently, he was forced to consider a psychogenic cause—that traumatic dreams and other symptoms served the function of helping the traumatized individual master the terrifying event by working it over and over in the victim's mind.

The persistently annoying failure of medical science to discover any definitive organic basis for these debilitating stress syndromes led to a gradual acceptance of psychological explanations, as the Freudian influence began to be felt more generally throughout psychiatry. This contributed to the replacement of shell shock by the more mentalistic-sounding term, *war neurosis*.

With this conceptual leap, physicians now no longer felt compelled to tie their diagnoses and treatments to unobservable defects of nervous tissue. Accordingly, Ferenczi and his colleagues (1921) elaborated the basic model of traumatic neurosis that is still largely accepted today among psychodynamic theorists (Horowitz, 1986). Ferenczi's group described the central role of anxiety, the persistence of morbid apprehension, regression of the ego, the attempted reparative function of recurring nightmares, and the therapeutic use of ventilation and understanding of the trauma. For the most part, the patients themselves seemed to do well with the kinds of psychologically expressive and supportive therapies that were provided by caring counselors, ministers, or doctors.

Continuing research and clinical experience expanded the theoretical base of trauma psychology. After surveying over a thousand reports in the international literature published during the First World War, Southard (1919) concluded that shell shock, war neurosis, and similar syndromes were primarily psychological syndromes. Kardiner (1941) followed a group of patients with war neuroses for more than a decade and concluded that severe war trauma produced a constriction of the ego that prevented these patients from adapting to and mastering life's subsequent challenges. Kardiner elaborated a conceptualization of trauma termed *psychoneurosis* that is quite close to the modern concept of post-traumatic stress disorder (see Chapter 8). The features of Kardiner's physioneurosis included: persistence of a startle response or irritability, proneness to explosive behavior, fixation on the trauma, an overall constriction of the personality, and a disturbed dream life, including vivid nightmares.

The experiences of the Second World War contributed surprisingly little to the development of new theories and treatments for wartime trauma, except for its redubbing as *battle fatigue.* In fact, resistance to the very concept of battle fatigue, with it's implications of mental weakness and lack of moral resolve, was widespread in both medical and military circles. There was a war on, plenty of good Joes were getting killed and wounded, and the army had little sympathy for the whinings of a few slackers and nervous nellies who couldn't buck up and pull their weight.

However, it was becoming apparent that wartime psychological trauma could take place in circumstances other than the actual battlefield. In WWII, then Korea and Vietnam, and most recently in the Persian Gulf wars, clinicians began to learn about disabling stress syndromes associated with large-scale bombings of civilian populations, prisoner of war and concentration camps, "brainwashing" of POW's, civilian atrocities, terrorism, and the threat of wholesale nuclear annihilation.

Today's daily media relentlessly continue to churn out more than ample examples of every imaginable species of human tragedy: war crimes, industrial injuries, plane crashes, auto accidents, rapes, assaults, domestic violence, child abuse, earthquakes, hurricanes, fires, floods, toxic spills, terrorist bombings—the list goes on (Miller, 1994b, 1998b, 1998c, 1998d, 1999c, 2002a, 2002b, 2004b, in press-e). In 1980, traumatic stress syndromes were finally codified as an identifiable type of psychopathological syndrome—*posttraumatic stress disorder* (PTSD)—in the American Psychiatric Association's official *Diagnostic and Statistical Manual of Mental Disorders* (APA, 1980) and remains there in the current edition (APA, 2000). In law enforcement and emergency services, this became incorporated into the concept of *critical incident stress* (Mitchell & Everly, 1996, 2003), and some authorities have gone so far as to characterize police trauma as the psychological aftermath of "civilian combat" (Violanti, 1999). This will be discussed further in Chapter 8.

Psychophysiology and Neuropsychology of Stress and Stress Syndromes

Of course, we know today that the mental and the physical are not separate categories: we think and feel with our brains and we react with our bodies—how could it be otherwise? Accordingly, over the last century, clinicians began to see the workings of the mind and body as interlocking sets of self-regulating systems. The modern study of the psychophysiology of stress is generally regarded as beginning with Claude Bernard's (1865) concept of the *milieu internal,* a term he used to describe the self-regulating mechanism that every healthy organism utilizes to maintain a constant state of adaptive functioning. This equilibrium can be disrupted by stress or disease, but as long as the organism survives, it will endeavor to restore and maintain this optimal internal state.

In the early 20th century, Walter Cannon (1914, 1939) used the term *homeostasis* to refer also to a state of biological equilibrium that could be derailed by stress, but that the organism would attempt to re-regulate back into health. Cannon also urged physicians to consider the effects of psychological stress on physiological functioning, ushering in the modern study of psychosomatic illness (Alexander, 1950; Weiner, 1977, 1992).

Probably the most well-known account of the stress response comes from the work of Hans Selye (1956, 1973, 1975) whose active research spanned the decades from the 1930's to the 1970's. Selye developed the concept of the *general adaptation syndrome,* or GAS, which he believed to define the physiological response to stressors of almost every type—from infections and toxins to social stress and interpersonal power struggles. Selye's GAS is said to consist of three overlapping, but distinct stages.

In the *stage of alarm,* the organism marshals its physiological resources to cope with the stressor. For Selye, this involves activation of the hypothalamo-pituitary-adrenal axis, resulting in the increased production of cortisol by the adrenal cortex. This hormone has an anti-inflammatory effect on the body and also has neuroactive and psychoactive effects on the brain. The alarm-stage stress response also mobilizes the sympathetic nervous system and increases secretion of adrenalin from the adrenal medulla.

In the *stage of resistance,* the body goes into a kind of extended overdrive, as all systems stay on high alert while the organism is coping with the stressor, which may be anything from a bad flu to a bad divorce. In the best case, the organism rallies and the crisis is eventually passed, with the individual becoming more resilient in the process. In this case, Nietzsche (1969) is right: "Whatever doesn't kill me makes me stronger." Indeed, in some instances, adaptive responding to stress can lead to *transcendent coping* and *post-traumatic growth* (Calhoun & Tedeschi, 1999; Tedeschi & Calhoun, 1995, 2004; Tedeschi & Kilmer, 2005).

But no organism can stay on red alert forever. If the crisis is not resolved, at some point the organism reaches the *stage of exhaustion,* in which physiological reserves are finally depleted and the organism begins to deteriorate and may even die. Sorry, Nietzsche, but in this case, "Whatever doesn't kill me . . . can make me really, really sick."

More recent research has revealed that the stress response may be more graded and nuanced, depending on the individual. For example, Dienstbier (1989) has used the term *toughness* to refer to a distinct reaction pattern to stress—mental, emotional, or physiological—that characterizes animals and humans who cope effectively with stress (Miller, 1989, 1990, 1998a). Two main physiological systems underlie the toughness response.

The first involves a pathway from the brain's hypothalamus to the sympathetic branch of the autonomic nervous system, and from there to the adrenal medulla. The sympathetic nervous system, or SNS, is responsible for the heart-pounding, fight-or-flight response that mobilizes body and mind to deal with challenging situations. As part of this response, the adrenal gland releases its main hormone, adrenalin.

The second system involved in the toughness response also begins with the hypothalamus but acts through the pituitary gland which in turn stimulates the adrenal cortex to release cortisol—the chief stress hormone involved in Selye's triphasic

GAS response. Together, the pattern of SNS-adrenal medulla and pituitary-adrenal cortex responses to stressful challenges characterizes the nature of the toughness trait.

It is the flexibility and gradedness of response of these two interrelated systems that defines an individual's physiological resilience or toughness. In resiliently tough organisms—animal or human—the normal, everyday activity of the two systems is low and modulated; tough individuals are at relative ease under most ordinary circumstances and their physiological responses reflect this relative quiescence. But when faced with a stressful challenge or threat, the SNS-adrenal medulla system springs into action quickly and efficiently, while the pituitary-adrenal cortex system remains relatively stable. As soon as the emergency is over, the adrenalin response returns quickly to normal, while the cortisol response stays low. The smoothness and efficiency of the physiological arousal pattern is what characterizes the psychophysiological toughness response—a response that has important aftereffects on the brain. Such a restrained reaction prevents depletion of catecholamines, important brain neurotransmitters that affect mood and motivation.

Not so with the untough. The physiological reactions of less resilient individuals tend to be excessive and longer-lasting, even in the face of everyday hassles. The result is more intense and disorganizing arousal, less effective coping, and faster depletion of brain catecholamines, which can lead to helplessness and depression. With each tribulation, major or minor, less resilient individuals tend to over-respond, their arousal levels overwhelming them, and rendering them unable to do much about the current situation, leading to little confidence in their future ability to cope.

That's where the real psychological significance of psychophysiological toughness comes in. Humans can do one thing animals can't: we can reflect on our own thoughts, feelings, and actions, conceptualize our responses in terms of what kind of person that makes us, and thereby anticipate how we'll react to future challenges. Dienstbier (1989) points out that the toughness response—or its absence—interacts with a person's psychological appraisal of his or her own ability to cope with challenge.

This in turn contributes to the person's self-image as an effective master of adversity or a helpless reactor—a self-assessment that influences later psychophysiological reactions to stress.

This, then, is the psychophysiological rationale of the MET-TLE program: By learning to control your perceptions, feelings, thoughts, and reactions in advance, through progressive practice and rehearsal, and in combination with your operational training, you will develop that core of resilient toughness—your psychological body armor—that will enable you to face any challenge with improved confidence and effectiveness. You can forget the biology lesson if you want to. The important thing to remember is that, although individuals differ naturally in their innate resilience, just as they do in physical strength, virtually any officer can reinforce their psychological body armor and ramp up their toughness skills by following and *practicing* the guidelines in this book.

Types of Crisis

As we'll see throughout this book, stress management and crisis intervention are inextricably linked (Miller, 2006*l*). Different types and sources of crisis can affect both the personal lives of police officers and the work they do with citizens (Anderson et al, 1995; Toch, 2002). These can be differentiated into several categories, although, as with most naturalistic classifications, several types overlap and blend together.

Personal crises involve family, friends, and significant others. Examples include relationship problems, separation and divorce, parent-child conflict, financial strains, alcohol and drug problems, and stresses within the extended family. At the extremes, these may express themselves in the form of child abuse, domestic violence, stalking and harassment, or suicide. Many of these behaviors may be fueled by alcohol or drug abuse.

Professional crises involve stresses related to work. Examples include management-employee conflicts, harassment by coworkers, filing of grievances, and stresses related to discipline, termination, or downsizing. Extreme cases may escalate to sexual harassment and workplace violence.

Situational crises refer to specific, short-term crises that may vary in severity, but are time-limited in nature, even though they may have long-term effects. There are numerous examples of these in almost everybody's life, including bereavement of family members, traumatic termination of a relationship or job, accidental injury, financial pinches, legal hassles, workplace rivalries, or the effects of natural disasters.

Ongoing crises are, by definition, longer in duration and may have an abrupt onset, such as an injury that produces long-term disability or a criminal charge or civil lawsuit that is followed by years of legal wrangling. Or the crisis may evolve more gradually, such as a progressive physical or mental illness, or an escalating series of financial losses.

Again, the boundaries between categories are fluid. A situational crisis of job loss may become an ongoing financial crisis if alternative employment can't be found in a sagging economy. An ongoing problematic relationship can escalate to violence when prodded by lack of money and family budget squabbles that result from the job loss. Violence can lead to arrest, incurring further financial losses and heightening family stress, and so on. How people cope with these types of crises depends on the nature and intensity of the crisis itself, the coping resources of the individuals involved, and the practical and psychosocial support systems available.

Types of Prevention: The Psychoepidemiology of Crisis Management

Epidemiology is the clinical science that studies the spread of illnesses and their effects within populations. Most familiar in the area of infectious disease, the epidemiological model has also been applied to a range of physical and psychological disorders, from the mortality in neighborhoods exposed to a virulent influenza infection, to posttraumatic stress disorder in workplaces affected by a workplace violence incident. Epidemiologists distinguish three main stages of prevention, which are termed primary, secondary, and tertiary prevention. These can also be applied to psychological casualties and disabilities within a population, as well as to individual cases of crisis intervention work (Gilliland & James, 1993; Miller, 1998d).

The goal of *primary prevention* is to prevent as many new cases of the crisis as possible from arising in the first place. In the case of an impending flu epidemic, this might involve vaccinations for vulnerable members of the community, educational programs targeting cleanliness and hygiene for preventing infection, and improved public sanitation and school nutrition programs to bolster physical health and resistance. For impending mental health crises, for example, dealing with potential workplace violence, this might involve public information about practical prevention measures for identifying and defusing threats, education about the nature of workplace bullying and harassment, and the stress syndromes they entail, diversity training, stress management and conflict resolution skills, and training in how to recognize the warning signs of impending violence.

Secondary prevention assumes that there has already been an initial outbreak of the crisis within the population. The goal is now to prevent it from spreading further and to minimize its effects. In our flu epidemic example, some individuals may have already been infected. Some of the secondary prevention measures will now involve improving and extending the measures taken in primary prevention, as well as instituting new ones, such as making doubly sure others are fully immunized, and if necessary, taking such drastic measures as quarantining contagious persons. For a brewing workplace violence crisis, we might recognize that an employee or customer is becoming increasingly agitated and has already threatened one or more persons and perhaps destroyed some property. At this stage, we would try to de-escalate the conflict, contain and isolate the subject, call police or security, and begin evacuating nearby employees from the area if necessary.

In *tertiary prevention*, the crisis has hit its peak or run its course, and what we are actually "preventing" at this stage is the development or worsening of effects that might occur in the aftermath. For the flu, this may involve treating secondary bacterial infections or malnutrition syndromes in flu survivors whose immune systems have been weakened, arranging care for children of dead or disabled parents, and maintaining electricity, food, and sanitation in affected areas. For the workplace violence crisis, this might mean arranging mental health follow-up to limit the development of post-traumatic stress reactions among affected employees and customers, as well as dealing with the media and general public to restore the organization's reputation and image so that the company's viability is not destroyed by the episode.

The overall concept is that most crises are fluid, organic entities that evolve over a time course—which can range from minutes to years—and that, at each stage, there must be an established set of measures to counteract the traumatic effects of the crisis. Hence, preparation, planning, and training are crucial.

Guiding Principles of Stress Management and Crisis Intervention

The following principles have evolved out of my own work in police psychology, and grows out of my broader experience in stress management and crisis intervention in a wide variety of setting, including law enforcement and emergency service agencies, schools and workplaces, and medical and mental health facilities (Miller, 1994b, 1995, 1998b, 1998c, 1998d, 1999a, 1999b, 1999c, 1999d, 2000a, 2000b, 2000c, 2002a, 2002b, 2004b, 2006l, in press-b, in press-c, in press-d, in press-e). If many of these principles sound familiar, that's because they relate to the practical psychology that most law enforcement officers already employ.

The Best Form of Crisis Intervention is Crisis Prevention

Recalling the principles of primary, secondary, and tertiary prevention, it is clear that *the best way to handle a crisis is to prevent it from happening in the first place.* Hardly a day goes by in police work that opportunities for staving off crises do not occur. In fact, police officers may actually have a unique advantage over other emergency service professionals in this regard. Firefighters and paramedics are, by definition, responders to emergencies that have already begun—a fire in a toxic chemical plant or an auto accident with injuries, for example. These professionals can react, but they usually can't predict, anticipate, or prevent.

The patrol function of police officers, however, places them in a unique position to see trouble coming and to take action before it boils over to a critical level of harm or a dangerous confrontation. Of course, not every law enforcement crisis can be anticipated or averted, but those officers who are uniquely successful in their jobs seem to have a talent for keeping problems under control, yet are able to take assertive action when necessary. How to use communication strategies to defuse conflicts before they erupt into crisis situations is covered in depth elsewhere (Miller, 2006l) and will also be the subject of a forthcoming volume in this series. The present book will give you the tools you need to stay focused and effective in the face of a critical emergency and to recover quickly and healthily.

All Successful Crisis Intervention Involves Crisis Prevention

This is the corollary to the above principle. Again, the principles of primary, secondary, and tertiary prevention imply that it is virtually never too late to intervene successfully in a crisis and prevent further harm, disability, or trauma from occurring. Further, in the real world, the three kinds of prevention are fluid and overlapping concepts. For example, talking two intoxicated citizens out of a brawl primarily prevents them from incurring physical injuries or legal charges. Quickly breaking up the fight once they have grabbed each other and tussled on the ground secondarily prevents them from racking up more serious arrestable charges and from incurring more than scrapes and bruises, while at the same time primarily prevents bystanders from becoming involved and being arrested or injured themselves.

If one combatant stabs the other with a knife or bashes him over the head with a bottle, restraining and arresting the assailant and calling for paramedic and additional police backup secondarily prevents the victim from being killed by another blow or stab wound, while primarily preventing injury to the officer from a now-clearly violent subject. Finally, how the arrest is handled, and making sure one or more officers remain on-scene after the melee is over to reassure frightened or angry citizens that the officers' actions were justifiable and in the interest of public safety, represents tertiary prevention of a potential civil disturbance or of smoldering community animosity arising from the original brawl and the police action that breaks it up.

Stress Management and Crisis Intervention are Interrelated

As noted throughout this book, it is a principle of my overall approach to law enforcement training (Miller, 2006*l*) that stress management cannot be separated from crisis intervention, as each comprises an essential component of the other. Crises are most likely to arise under conditions of stress, and that stress is almost always further exacerbated by the very crises they provoke. It's all about vicious cycles—and what you can do to turn them into positive cycles. Stress provokes and exacerbates crises; crises elevate stress. Effective crisis intervention reduces stress, which in turn makes crisis management easier. Officers who know how to manage their own stress are less likely to be goaded or baited into escalating a citizen confrontation into a crisis, and will be better able to use clear thinking and effective action if a crisis unavoidably occurs.

Therefore, effective stress management *is* an important crisis intervention skill, a form of primary prevention, as discussed above. Whether the stresses involve citizens in an officer's patrol area or hassles and crises in the officer's own life, learning to deal constructively with life's challenges reinforces the psychophysiological toughness response and constitutes a primary layer of the psychological body armor that is vital for deflecting the worst consequences of a stressful critical incident or life challenge.

Stress Management and
Crisis Intervention Principles are Universal

The mental toughness training principles of stress management and crisis intervention should be seen as broad-purpose skills that can be applied to a wide range of crisis situations. This doesn't mean that one size fits all: training and experience are still required to be effective in any particular domain of law enforcement action—vehicle stop, suspect search, building entry, hostage negotiation, undercover work, and so on—since each domain contains distinct features and, indeed, each individual crisis will contain unique elements.

But just as emergency medical care for diverse injuries and illness (gunshot wound, heart attack, epileptic seizure) follows certain universal principles (assess vital signs, establish heart rhythm and airway, scan for internal injuries), so it is with emergency crisis intervention. This is all the more true inasmuch as one kind of crisis can easily transform into another: a domestic squabble turns into a hostage-barricade situation; a citizen dispute becomes a civil disturbance; a robbery-in-progress call flashes over into an assault-of-officer or suicide-by-cop episode. Mastering the stress management and crisis intervention skills in this book will enable you to handle a broad range of law enforcement and other life crisis situations.

20/20 Hindsight = 20/20 Insight = 20/20 Foresight

20/20 hindsight has gotten a bum rap, as it is often equated with second-guessing, Monday-morning quarterbacking, or useless self-flagellation. But in reality, looking back on an unsuccessful action, analyzing it, and trying to learn from it is an absolutely essential process for developing any skill—*if* the hindsight analysis leads to a certain degree of insight into what went wrong and how it happened. This insight into what happened last time can then be used to create a new set of options and action plans for next time. What we're talking about is the whole concept of *learning from experience* and developing *expertise* which will be more fully discussed in the next chapter.

In fact, this 20/20/20 principle is used all the time in law enforcement, emergency services, and the military, under the heading of *operational debriefing.* Within law enforcement, it is an essential component of hostage negotiation team training and undercover operations, to cite two examples (Miller, 2005e, 2006j). Indeed, all responsible professionals engage in an ongoing process of continuing education and self-improvement—a *culture of knowledge* (Miller, 2006*l*)—and the present volume is intended to contribute to that process.

Learning Never Stops, or "It's The Training, Stupid" (ITTS)

Nobody is born knowing anything. Consistent with the 20/20/20 principle, all the natural skill and talent in the world won't make you an expert in any area, unless you develop and train that talent to the fullest extent possible. Consider the professional athlete, artist, or musician (Hays & Brown, 2004). Certainly, without a natural gift for his or her sport or skill, training alone won't take the individual past their upper limit of capability. But raw talent alone is insufficient: the athlete or performer has to work at developing that skill to its ultimate level in order to attain excellence and stay in that upper one-percent zone, to continue to push the envelope. Indeed, *the best form of stress management is proper training and knowledge* because the more automatic, flexible, and generalized a particular area of skill and expertise, the less surprised and overwhelmed you'll be in any situation. More on this in Chapter 2.

In fact, research shows that those individuals at the very top of their game never coast; if anything, they actually put in many times more effort than those with less innate talent. That is, they take what's great and devote extraordinary effort to making it greater (Briggs, 1988; Buckingham & Coffman, 1999; Simonton, 1994). That's why one of this book's guiding principles is that, for true professionals in any field, learning, training, and teaching never stop. In the *culture of knowledge* (Miller, 2006*l*), we keep growing and, as we do so, we contribute to the growth of our colleagues, our organization, and our profession. To that end, this book will serve as a guide for police officers, and the mental health clinicians who assist them, in developing the flexible mental toughness skills needed to manage the extreme stresses, crises, and dangers that law enforcement work can entail. But what exactly *is* mental toughness? It is to this that we now turn.

2

The Essential Components of Mental Toughness: The METTLE Model

Most people would describe their jobs as stressful to some degree. Yet, in only a few professions—police, emergency services, disaster management, the military—does this stress literally involve making critical decisions in life-and-death situations.

That's why most "stress management" programs you've encountered probably have tended to focus almost exclusively on mental and physical calming and other low arousal techniques to prepare for and deal with the aftermath of a stressful experience. Far less attention has been paid to training emergency responders to manage stress *during* a critical life-and-death encounter. And even fewer programs utilize the full range of physiological, cognitive, and behavioral self-management tools to deal effectively with the types of extreme life-and-death crises that occur in law enforcement work.

Yet stress management in critical situations has been applied to a number of high-demand performance areas, from law enforcement, to emergency services, to athletics, to show business—all professions where maintaining peak efficiency under conditions of extreme stress is crucial. Furthermore, being able to display such grace under pressure is a key ingredient in the field of *performance enhancement,* which enables soldiers, police officers, emergency responders, professional athletes, and entertainment performers to exert their personal best under conditions of extreme stress and competition (Hays & Brown, 2004; Maynard, 2003; Scanff & Taugis, 2002; Thelwell & Greenless, 2001, 2003; Thelwell et al, 2006).

Like any skill, research suggests that mental toughness can be both a natural and a developed phenomenon—usually a combination of both. There will always be large individual differences in people's innate potential for any skill or talent, whether physical or mental. A naturally beefy guy who takes up bodybuilding is going to end up with a far huger muscle mass and be able to bench press way more poundage than his naturally skinny friend who follows him to the gym and trains just as hard. But the skinny guy's job is not to become another Arnold—it's to develop *his own* potential to its utmost: to become as hard and sinewy and wiry as his genetics will let him, and thereby earn the genuine respect of his fellow sportsmen for making the most of what he's got.

The same principle applies to virtually any skill where natural ability and intense training combine to produce varying levels of proficiency across individuals—from basketball to ballet, sharpshooting to surgery. And this talent-training combo certainly includes the ability to learn and use mental toughness skills in critical situations. There will always be those who naturally excel, but almost anyone can increase their efficiency significantly. And in a potentially lethal encounter, even a narrow margin of improvement in mental toughness and reaction efficiency may be the crucial decimal point that saves your life.

Also remember that mental toughness is not just one entity, but is composed of a number of separate yet interrelated elements, and different people may excel at some elements more than others. Some people may have a natural talent for regulating arousal level (Chapter 3) but be less gifted at modulating attention (Chapter 4). Others may be natural masters of visualization and imagery (Chapter 5) but need far more work at using self-talk or cognitive restructuring (Chapter 6). The key to success is to punch up the skills you're weak in while, at the same time, maximizing your strong points to their fullest (Buckingham & Coffman, 1999; Collins, 2001; Hays & Brown, 2004).

As noted above, the kinds of Mental Toughness Training skills you will learn in this book take part of their background from the performance enhancement field in sports and other areas of competitive performance. Accordingly, this chapter will borrow and adapt from a variety of performance domains to develop a practical model of mental toughness that incorporates the following three essential components:

1. *Toughness:* Mental conditioning.
2. *Mastery:* Recognition-primed decision-making and expertise.
3. *Flow:* Smoothness and automaticity of performance, or "making it look easy" (even though it's not).

Toughness on the Field: Mental Conditioning in Competitive Sports

From the time of ancient Sparta, when athletic competition served as actual preparation for warfare, sports have always represented a form of ritualized combat (Sherman, 2005)—that's why we take it so damn seriously. So it's not surprising that much of the research and practical advice on mental toughness comes from the domain of *sports psychology* (Bull et al, 2005; Goldberg, 1998; Gould et al, 1987; Jones. et al, 2002; Loehr, 1995; Thelwell et al, 2005). In reviewing this literature, I have been able to distill the diverse components and conceptual constructs of this field down to four primary qualities that characterize mental toughness in sports and that, most importantly for our purposes, are of key relevance to law enforcement applications of mental toughness training. These are (1) confidence; (2) motivation; (3) focus; and (4) resilience.

Confidence

A professional athlete or performer puts his or her fundamental self on the line with every game or performance. Excellent performers don't just do their craft, they *are* their craft. This orientation is probably familiar to those police officers, doctors, soldiers, athletes, and others who view their occupations as more akin to a calling than a job. This takes *confidence*. Within sports psychology, a recent shift in philosophy proposes that an athlete should develop a sense of *personal excellence*—a strong personal identity with clear morals and character—simultaneously with *performance excellence* (Hays & Brown, 2004).

Confident athletes have an unshakable belief in their own abilities and, more pointedly, that these abilities are up to the task of beating their opponent. They thrive on the pressure of competition because they possess the skills and temperament to cope adaptively with the stresses and anxieties of competition. Their resoluteness cannot be shaken by the performance or intimidation of the other players. Confident athletes are able to overcome their inevitable self-doubts by a variety of coping mechanisms, many of which will be described in this book.

Confident athletes are independent and take responsibility for themselves. This responsibility includes not just their game performance but their commitment to their own excellence and self-development. They are able to honestly and critically self-appraise their own performance, to work on correcting their weak spots and give themselves credit for all the good work that they do. They compete with themselves to constantly improve their own performance. Their confidence is stable and unbreakable precisely because it is based on a track record of honest appraisal and continual training (recall Chapter 1) that allows them to draw strength from their own physical conditioning which, in turn, generates further confidence, in a positive cycle.

But confidence does not come from empty "self-esteem." It must be based on a record of real accomplishment, otherwise it is merely bloated narcissism (Doss, 2006). In fact, psychologist Alfred Bandura's (1977, 1986) *self-efficacy theory* supports the view that a person's confidence is most influenced by prior efforts and accomplishments. After the activity is completed, there is a kind of self-reflective feedback loop of performance assessment and this in turn influences further performance— much like the 20/20/20 principle described in Chapter 1. In this model, dealing constructively with negative outcomes becomes a crucial part of the process.

Confidence is more than just a good feeling—it is vital to performance. The development of positive performance expectations is a crucial factor in preparing personnel to operate under high-demand conditions (Locke et al, 1984; Salas et al,

1996). For example, an examination of specialized hazardous duty training given to British military bomb-disposal experts showed that those who developed positive performance expectations reported relatively little fear during operations (Rachman, 1983). In short, attitude does matter.

Motivation

While confidence sustains the athlete's performance, *motivation* spurs it forward. Obviously, confidence and motivation are reciprocal and mutually reinforcing: motivation impels performance which builds confidence which further increases motivation and so on.

Motivated athletes have an insatiable desire to succeed and excel, a desire that comes from within and cannot be compelled or coerced. Even if they acknowledge that they're not necessarily the most naturally gifted, they are determined to make the most of their abilities, to develop them to the utmost, to *self-actualize* in Maslow's (1968) terminology. They are willing to take risks— not in the sense of recklessness, but in terms of stretching their abilities and embracing new challenges. They believe that they can make a unique contribution to their team and to their sport, that they can "make a difference." This, of course, is tied up with the professional identity factor noted above.

For motivated athletes, the pressure of competition only heightens their drive to succeed (Hayes & Brown, 2004). They have developed a "never-say-die" mindset that allows them to weather and withstand performance setbacks and career ups and downs. They can tie short-term performance to long-term goals in order to sustain their motivation over bad stretches because they are committed to their craft for the long haul. Their motivation also produces a powerful work ethic that impels them to "go the extra mile" in training and practice; they never coast, they're always moving forward. They compete with themselves as well as with others. As noted above for confidence, motivation must be based on reality, and these athletes use their stumbles and failures as learning experiences to do better next time—i.e. the 20/20/20 rule.

Focus

If motivation is the fuel that drives the performance engine, *focus* is the guidance system that allows the engine to stay on track toward the athlete's goals. Many observers have commented on the fierce concentration shown by athletes both in training and during the actual game, a "positive tunnel vision" that enables them to zero in on their goals and sustain motivation over time.

As used here, the term *focus* has two meanings: focus on the moment-to-moment, here-and-now aspects of a particular training exercise or performance, and a more long-term, event-spanning focus on career goals.

Being fully focused on a particular performance task enables the athlete to persevere in the face of internal and external distractions, whether related to the sport itself or to extraneous matters. The skilled athlete can also change the intensity and direction of this focus as needed, and Chapter 4 will describe how to flexibly manipulate the faculty of attention for maximal focus on the task at hand.

Focus is also internal, and skilled athletes have learned to monitor their inner physical and mental states, to be able to run a self-system check as needed, both to assess ongoing performance during a competition and to check themselves between performances. This self-focus also extends to short- and long-term goals. More broadly, it also refers to a balance between being focused on the needs of the team (in team sports) and the needs and goals of the athlete him- or herself. Self-focus also refers to honest self-appraisal, as well as to the ability to keep perspective on both successes and failures, so that confidence is not inappropriately inflated or degraded.

Focus also includes clarity of thinking, and many athletes will describe states of almost supernatural mental sharpness during intense competitions. This comes about through intensive and protracted training, so that when critical situations arise, the athlete is not overwhelmed by anxiety and complexity, but can switch into a smooth, efficient performance mode as needed. One component of clear thinking is good decision-making, which involves being able to make the right choice at the right time with confidence, especially when the pressure is on at a critical moment in the competition. As will be discussed shortly, this ability to quickly choose an effective course of action is vital to command decision-making under stress.

Sometimes focus can have an intensity component that is essential for getting military troops through a tough spot. Regehr & Bober (2004) describe how Lieutenant General Romero Dallaire, who led the Canadian peacekeeping mission during the Rwandan genocide, devised a simple but direct method for helping his troops deal with the inhumane and horrific scenarios they had to confront: keep them working till they drop. The idea was to ensure that the troops didn't even have time to think about the reality of what they were seeing and doing, so they could put the emotional reaction on hold by immersion in the task itself. Nevertheless, he states, when certain individuals reached a point where they could no longer function effectively and were on the verge of becoming psychological casualties, they were respectfully and honorably relieved of duties and sent home. This was done both for the well-being of the individual and to ensure that their distress did not permeate the rest of the troops and impede the group's ability to continue their grueling and gruesome work.

While this approach may seem like cruel slave-driving, it was actually an opportunity for these military professionals to show their best in an event, horrifying and tragic though it may be, that they had prepared and trained for their whole careers. This, in essence, was the "big one." It thus had the potential of becoming a shining moment in a soldier's career, the chance to use all of one's personal and professional skills and energies in the helping, investigating, and recovery work that characterizes this kind of man-made disaster. The team and the work came together at a pivotal challenging time. For law enforcement officers, the same orientation is often seen in hostage negotiation, SWAT, riot control, disaster management, and other incidents where training and extreme events coalesce to produce a life-and-death crisis that officers are called upon to handle and overcome.

Resilience

One important message of this book is that toughness is flexible, not fixed, resilient, not rigid. *Resilience* is the bounce-back that enables skilled athletes and other professionals to endure and prevail over physical injuries, mental shocks, and performance failures without burning out or melting down. The analogy is to a piece of tough industrial rubber that can conform and distort its shape under pressure, but will never shatter or rupture. Hard wood or solid steel are technically "stronger" than rubber, but either one ultimately has its breaking point. Rubber bends and twists, but it always comes back.

Resilient athletes don't fold under pressure. They adapt to extreme conditions by using their training and experience to devise and implement moment-to-moment corrections of their performance in response rapidly changing circumstances. Even when knocked for a loop, they quickly regain equilibrium and self-control without being overwhelmed. They can endure physical pain and emotional distress and maintain technique and sustained effort by what seems to be sheer force of will, but which is really a tough resilience that grows out of confidence and determination borne of training, perseverance, and expertise.

Again, the core components of mental toughness are reciprocal and interactive. Resilience partly depends on confidence which, in turn, is based on a track record of accomplishment. Specifically with law enforcement, Doss (2006) notes that when an officer's confidence is degraded because of poor training or a negative outcome despite utilizing techniques he thought would work, this may have a deteriorative effect on subsequent performance and the recovery process may be painfully slow. This explains the seemingly obsessive nature of training that characterizes all high-performance fields. Proper training not only helps build skill and proficiency itself, it also helps inoculate the professional against corrosive self-doubt and feelings of failure in the case of a bad outcome, because intense training enhances the 20/20/20 process which further increases confidence (Miller, 2006*l*).

Part of maintaining resilience is taking care of the "machine." Most cops wouldn't think of going into the field with shoddy or untested equipment, but many will ignore and neglect the maintenance needs of their own minds and bodies (Garner, 2005). The various kinds of performers interviewed and studied by Hays & Brown (2004) are all professionals at the top of their games, earning their living by providing consistently high-quality performance on a regular basis, and their methods of self-care are tailored to the unique demands of their specific performance domain. In the business arena, performers count on the sharpness of their mental skills; for athletes and performing artists, their bodies are most central to performance. For law enforcement officers, whose jobs involve a unique combination of communicative skill and decisive and forceful action, virtually every aspect of their mind and body becomes a precision instrument that must be kept in peak condition.

Recognition-Primed Decision-Making and Expertise

In the cool, logical world of the academic classroom or corporate boardroom, decisions are usually made by a dispassionate, logical, step-by-step process: first access all the relevant information, then weigh the evidence carefully, and finally come up with a balanced spreadsheet of risks and benefits to guide the appropriate decision. But in the real world of emergency crisis management, decision makers have to think on their feet, shoot from the hip, fly by the seat of their pants—well, you get the idea. Decision-making in such naturalistic settings is characterized by several important features (Klein, 1993; Orasanu & Connolly, 1993).

First, the goals are typically ill-defined and the tasks poorly structured. When arriving on the scene of an unfolding crisis, it's rarely immediately clear what is the correct action to take. Instead, important chunks of information will be missing, and what is available may be incomplete, ambiguous, or just plain wrong. Think of what transpires in the first few minutes of a major chemical spill, freeway traffic pileup, or hostage-barricade crisis.

Second, the conditions and requirements of the situation are usually not static, but may shift from moment to moment, as the crisis continues to unfold and more data trickle in. This is where the thinking-on-one's-feet dimension really comes into play. The seat-of-the-pants component involves making rapid adjustments and course corrections to changing circumstances in real-time, a process of implementing *action feedback loops.*

Complicating the above factors are the super-high adrenalin levels inherent in most emergency situations. The stakes are often life and death, and the time pressure is intense, as decisions must be arrived at, implemented, and/or changed at a moment's notice.

Further, these plans and directives must often be communicated to multiple members of the response team, many of whom may be in different locations and not immediately accessible. By the time an instruction reaches one team member, the plans may have already changed or new information may have already come in.

Finally, on-scene command decision makers must be mindful of the broader implications of their actions for their agency and the community at large. In any large-scale event, there will inevitably be media attention and after-the-fact second-guessing.

In response to conditions like these, cognitive psychology has examined how effective decision makers operate under conditions of chaos and confusion. Converging sources of research data and practical experience have identified a process called *recognition-primed decision-making,* or RPDM (Klein, 1989, 1993, 1996, 1998), which is uniquely concerned with rapid decision-making in complex, naturalistic, messy, real-time settings. RPDM is a fundamental component of what is commonly called *expertise* and has been studied in fields as diverse as chess, medicine, law practice, teaching, psychotherapy, physics, forensic science, military training, sports, performance arts, computer expertise, and salesmanship (Alba & Hitchinson, 1987; Chase & Simon, 1973; Chi et al, 1981; De Groot, 1965, 1966; Hays & Brown, 2004; Hedlund et al, 2003; Johnson et al, 1981, 1984; Leigh, 1987; Leigh & McGraw, 1989; Leinhardt & Greeno, 1986; Leong et al, 1989; Matsuo & Kusumi, 2002; Miller,

1993; Schraagen & Leijenhorst, 2001; Shepherd et al, 2006; Sternberg, 2002; Sujan et al, 1988; Szymanski, 1988).

In both critical and non-emergency situations, expert decision makers seem to invoke a cognitive strategy that doesn't require the kind of algorithmic, trial-and-error deduction that is typically taught in formal courses on logical reasoning and decision-making. Instead, by virtue of having accumulated a comprehensive storehouse of knowledge and experience, true experts rely on an almost instantaneous, holographic, at-a-glance kind of command decision-making that usually results in the right answer and the appropriate response to the challenge at hand. During crises, when there is a lot of activity and potential for confusion, RPDM is vital, and most effective command decision makers employ it intuitively (Bowers et al, 1996; Flin, 1996; Klein, 1988, 1989, 1993, 1996, 1998; Miller, 2005b, 2006i, 2006*l*; Orasanu & Backer, 1996; Orasanu & Connolly, 1993).

While RPDM has been studied for over a decade in the field of military and civilian emergency response (Flin, 1996; Klein, 1998), only recently has it begun to be applied specifically to day-to-day police work (Kavanaugh, 2006; Rossmo, 2006; Spaulding, 2005). As typically practiced in real-life settings, RPDM seems to consist of four overlapping phases: content knowledge, pattern matching, narrative generation, and decision-making. Although described here as a series of steps, to the actual on-scene decision maker, the RPDM process feels like an intuitive, seamless response rather than a stepwise comparison of alternative choices (Klein, 1993, 1998).

Content Knowledge

Knowledge is the foundation for mastery and expertise. There is no substitute for mastery of the skill domain that subsumes the expert's decision-making, whether this be sports, medicine, art, music, business, law, police work, or emergency response services. There is a general consensus that it takes at least ten years of intensive training and regular practice to attain elite performance in virtually every field studied (Ericsson et al, 1993).

This is called *content knowledge* and relates to one of the core principles from Chapter 1—ITTS: "It's the training, stupid." In a critical police situation, the officer's deep and broad knowledge and experience is marshaled by his or her brain instantaneously. The comparisons and weighing of factors that the current situation requires have all been done thousands of times in the past, in thousands of situations, either in real life, in simulation scenarios, or in independent study. These mental models of content knowledge, sometimes called *schemata* (Flin, 1996), represent stored templates of previous knowledge and experience which drive the rapid search for information when the expert is faced with a new situation.

So when the time comes for accurate knowledge to be applied to the present crisis, the decision maker's brain doesn't have to laboriously scroll down the list of available options until the right answer appears; instead, his or her brain quickly sizes up the situation and instantly "googles" the correct response. It may look like the decision maker is operating on a hunch, but it is really an instantaneous distillation of a vast storehouse of operational wisdom applied to the current situation. The prior training and experience make the response look "automatic."

Expert decision makers differ from novices in several fundamental ways. Their track record allows them to employ richer and more sophisticated mental models to guide their proactive data-seeking during critical incidents: they intuitively know what to look for and what to disregard or put on the back burner. Through their decade or more of training and experience, they have learned to seek both confirmatory and contradictory evidence as a check against overconfident responding (the 20/20/20 principle). As a result, their mental models are more intricate and allow them to perceive more complexity in the situation, to read the scene in finer-grained detail, to construct more comprehensive theories of the case, and thus better anticipate what could go wrong and what actions are likely to be right. Experts tend to store their memories and knowledge of tactical situations in the form of complex dynamic physical images, or "war stories."

This is not just for law enforcement or military operations. Expert salespeople, for example, have been shown to have richer and more overlapping knowledge bases concerning customers' product preferences and selling-related needs than beginners (Sujan et al, 1998). Leong et al (1989) found the selling scripts of higher-performing salespeople to be more distinctive than those of salespeople who performed less well. Matsuo & Kusumi (2002) found that the more experience salesperson's gain, the stronger the relationship between their content knowledge and their sales performance becomes. In an even more recent study, Shepherd et al (2006) found that expert salespeople tended to arrive at better problem-solving solutions and to be better able to relate to previous experiences in their problem-solving approach. Finally, expert salespeople were also found to be significantly faster and more confident in their decision-making approach. Similar findings have been reported in other fields.

Pattern Matching

In the thick of a crisis situation, experienced decision makers seem to concentrate on assessing and classifying the situation that presents itself. They can quickly size up details that may escape the novice, and integrate and make sense of the diverse data by a process called *pattern matching.* Once they recognize that they are dealing with a particular type of event, their knowledge-based intuitive RPDM springs into action and they are able to immediately identify the appropriate response to handle it. They perform a rapid mental feasibility study of the projected course of action, imagining how they would implement it, as an internal check on whether anything important might go wrong. If they envisage any problems, then the plan might be modified, but only if the entire original plan is rejected do they consider another strategy altogether. Again, bear in mind that this all takes place in a matter of seconds inside the decision maker's experienced head.

The game of chess is a time-honored mental metaphor for tactical military strategy and, during a competitive game, analysis has shown that true chess masters actually evaluate fewer alternative moves than do novices (De Groot, 1965, 1966). The experts invariably zero in on the strongest moves, with the best moves at the top of the list of alternatives. In contrast, weaker players seem to spend considerable time indiscriminately analyzing the consequences of multiple moves, including many bad ones. The explanation seems to be that, although the non-expert sees just an arrangement of pieces on the chessboard, the expert perceives any given arrangement as one variation of a game scenario already stored in memory (Chase & Simon, 1973). Thus, the important difference between experts and non-experts is in the quality, not quantity, of alternatives they generate. The expert's moves are sharper, more focused.

This has a tremendous effect on the speed and efficiency of decision-making and action because the expert's ability to immediately see new situations in terms of previously encountered alternatives enables him or her to almost instantaneously "know" the best next move at an almost automatic level (Johnson et al, 1984; Leinhardt & Greeno, 1986). By contrast, less experienced individuals take longer to formulate an initial response because they have fewer mental models to draw on, i.e. to pattern-match with (Chase & Simon, 1973). In real life medical crises, one emergency room physician (Hays & Brown, 2004) referred to the initial assessment of a situation as "gestalting," which he described as a rapid evaluation of the overall situation that enabled him to make fast and accurate triage assessments to save the maximum number of lives possible. This almost instantaneous knowledge of the right action to take in an emergency has obvious implications for police work.

Narrative Generation

In carrying out this internal mental evaluation, the command decision maker seems to intuitively combine all the relevant data to construct a plausible explanation for the situation. This internal narrative has been called *story building* (Klein, 1998; Pennington & Hastie, 1993), a concept adapted from legal research on juror psychology. In the present context of law enforcement emergency decision-making, this internal story building allows the officer to develop an almost instantaneous "theory of the case" to guide his or her subsequent actions. This is the use of a brief but deliberate mental simulation and evaluation to envision how the course of action might be carried out and to find potential difficulties that need to be avoided. This kind of anticipatory mental simulation is called *preplaying,* a kind of instant replay in reverse, that is, projecting the action forward in time and assessing its likely effect (Klein, 1996; Klein & Crandall, 1995).

For example, Flin (1996) has found that expert military commanders store their memories and knowledge of tactical scenarios in the form of complex dynamic physical images or "war stories," which also appears to be characteristic of expert emergency services commanders such as firefighters and paramedics. Similarly, expert forensic examiners have been found to develop a narrative about a given case that acts as a causal model to explain the presence or absence of evidence traces on the exhibits they examine (Schraagen & Leijenhorst, 2001). This guiding narrative storyline directs the forensic expert in his or her search process, helping to evaluate the relative importance of pieces of evidence, how and where to search for further relevant evidence, when to stop, and what traces to observe and record.

Decision-making

Having taken in the scene and pattern-matched a working mental model from stored content knowledge, in most real-life circumstances the expert will probably never have all the information or all the resources needed to make a decision that will ensure the guaranteed absolute best possible outcome. The expert's job, then, is not to optimize, but to *satisfice* (Flin, 1996; Klein, 1998), that is, to make the decision and implement the appropriate action that will control and stabilize the situation for right now—just enough for additional follow-up planning and implementation to take place later. In other words, sometimes you may not be able to turn the heat off at its source, but you may have to settle for keeping the lid on so the whole pot doesn't blow; this will buy time to search for the pilot light or fuel line when you get the chance. Another way to think of it is as a kind of first aid, like a splint to stabilize a shattered leg so the victim can at least hobble out of the burning building and get himself to the medical area where the wound can be treated.

This type of decision-making may require you to employ a process of internal, serial, mental generation and evaluation of options and to check them against their appropriate mental scenario—the story building, discussed above. Still, it's uncanny how, for knowledgeable and experienced expert decision makers, their first option usually proves to be the most workable one, that is, it satisfices. They can then use further incoming data to revise the plan as necessary and focus on elaborating and improving options for a successful outcome.

For example, in interviews with fireground commanders, Klein (1996; Klein et al, 1986) heard repeatedly that a mediocre choice, initiated in time, was better than an optimal choice that came too late. The biggest sin was failure to act. In operational settings—ranging from police emergency response, to disaster management, to military combat—there seem to be individual differences in a person's ability and readiness to process and act upon incomplete information. Just as brash impulsiveness carries clear penalties, so does a ploddingly reflective style that keeps searching for more and more information as the window of opportunity slams shut. The expert decision maker effects a mental compromise between premature closure that rules out effective action and delayed action that closes the proverbial barn door after the horse is gone.

In a comparison of expert and novice Israeli gunboat commanders using a computer-based, sea-combat task, Lipshitz & Ben Shaul (1997) found that the experts undertook a more efficient data search, collected more information before making a decision, "read" the situation more accurately, and made fewer bad decisions; that is, they made more efficient use of schemata and mental models to guide their decision-making—they were better satisficers.

Peak performance in the competitive business world can often involve a challenging blend of pre-performance strategy and adjustment to ongoing changes (Collins, 2001; Hays & Brown, 2004). A person may have an initial predetermined agenda, but ongoing assessment and feedback may necessitate dramatic modification of one's original plan. The ability to assess a situation both rapidly and accurately, and make necessary course-corrections in real-time, is the foundation of achieving excellence in high-performance settings.

A lawyer commented (Hays & Brown, 2004): "The key to what I do is *pace*. It's like using a clutch and an accelerator. Knowing enough to be quiet and listen and to try to really read what needs to happen. And then to take a stab at it. And still to listen, to figure out whether it worked or not, so that you don't over-commit too much to one way of doing it but are open to changing very quickly without appearing flighty" (p. 177). It's like a basketball player on the court or a fighter pilot in a dogfight—feinting and parrying to moment-by-moment critical changes in the ongoing game or battle.

Peak Performance Under Pressure: The "Flow" Experience

To outside observers, experts often make their tasks "look easy" and sometimes, by the experts' own self-description, the performance just seems to "take on a life of its own." Indeed, when one group of athletes described their greatest moment in sports (Ravizza, 1977), their responses contained the following elements: no fear of failure; no thinking of performance; total immersion in the activity; narrow focus of attention; a sense of effortlessness in producing action; a sense of being in complete control; disorientation of time and/or space; and experiencing a sense of "oneness" with the universe. Furthermore, these athletes described these greatest moments as being temporary and somehow beyond their voluntary control.

Although many authors have discussed the so-called *flow* experience as it pertains to athletics, the arts, business, communication, and personal relationships (Csikszentmihalyi, 1990; Jackson & Csikszentmihalyi, 1999; Privette & Bundrick, 1991; Williams & Krane, 1997), this concept has been specifically applied to the world of law enforcement and emergency services by Asken (1993) and Doss (2007). Whether called "flow," being in "the zone," or having a "peak experience," this sense of an almost transcendentally heightened performance has certain characteristics, familiar to anyone who has ever experienced it:

Fusion of action and awareness. There is a loss of self-consciousness as knowing flows into doing in one seamless process. The athlete's legs seem to run by themselves; the musician's piece seems to effortlessly issue forth from the instrument. The performer is "at one" with the experience.

Concentrated beam of attention. The performer is fully focused on the activity of importance and is able to tune out any extraneous distractions. Depending on the task, this beam of attention may vary from broad to narrow, and Chapter 4 will discuss specific techniques for learning to control attention.

Sense of control. There is a sublime self-confidence, a consummate sense of control over the situation and one's own actions. This is by no means a reckless disregard for danger or impulsive overconfidence, but rather a smooth, calm, and complete faith in one's ability to handle the challenge at hand.

Sense of purpose. There is no doubt or hesitation, and decisions seem easy.

Intrinsic motivation. An individual may embark on a law enforcement, military, athletic, or performance arts career for any number of purposes, such as money, prestige, and so on. However, during the critical activity itself, the only reason for doing it is that it *has* to be done; we *can't not* do it; we climb the mountain because "it's there." The joy is in the doing, and nobody has to persuade or force us to do what we love.

It bears repeating that the flow experience is predicated on a track record of training and practical exercise—the *content knowledge* discussed above—and occurs when physical and mental skills have been blended and rehearsed. The reason peak performances appear so effortless and to be operating "on instinct" is because they are not instinctual at all: they are so well-trained and practiced that the person has become a supreme exponent of that skill—"one with it," if you will. That's the kind of mastery you want to strive for in utilizing the mental toughness skills of this book.

Psychological Skills for Mental Toughness and Peak Performance in Law Enforcement

The three elements of *toughness, mastery,* and *flow* come together in the expert's pursuit of excellence and resilience to adversity in virtually every performance domain studied. Specifically for law enforcement and emergency services, Asken (1993) and Scanff & Taugis (2002) have described a set of skills that seem to correlate with the ability of a police officer or emergency service worker to exert peak performance in critical situations:

> *Commitment* refers to the officer's dedication to, and positive involvement with, his or her law enforcement work. The officer receives great satisfaction from doing a job well done, but without becoming unhealthily enmeshed to the point of overdependence on the police role to unilaterally bolster his or her personal identity.

> *Confidence* is the officer's belief—based on evidence from training, experience, and external performance appraisals—that he or she will have what it takes to handle an emergency situation when it arises.

> *Arousal control* is the skill that allows the officer to tone down the adrenalin rush that can lead to panicky decision-making and poor performance, as well as to pump up the emotional juice when flagging energy or motivation impedes optimum performance. The key is flexibility of arousal control, as will be discussed in Chapter 3.

> *Attention control* permits the officer to broadly scan the environment or focus attention on a specific feature as a consciously controlled process. Again, flexibility is the key, as discussed in Chapter 4.

Imagery is the ability of the officer to visualize himself performing well, to engage in a "virtual rehearsal" of his actions to instill a sense of mastery. More on this in Chapter 5.

Self-talk refers to the officer verbally guiding himself through a difficult task. The talk can either be instructional or motivational, but in either case serves as an "inner voice" for direction and encouragement. This is actually one component of a set of cognitive processing techniques discussed in Chapter 6.

Cognitive restructuring allows the officer to reframe negative events as opportunities for positive action. It is not denial of reality, but rather a creative exploration of options to counteract despair and pessimism when things are not going as expected. More on this in Chapter 6.

METTLE: Building a Better Toughness Model

The components of toughness, mastery, and flow translate into a model that can be utilized to develop and reinforce resilience and flexibility in the face of critical stress. Few of the concepts in this book are unique to the METTLE model itself; what the model does is integrate heretofore disparate elements from law enforcement psychology, military psychology, sports psychology, cognitive psychology, behavioral medicine, and stress management into a comprehensive training program for keeping your psychological body armor in peak working condition.

In turning next to the practice modules of the METTLE program in Chapters 3–7, you will note that they are presented as a series of steps to enhance cumulative learning. However, bear in mind that, in actual practice, the goal is for you to be able to use elements of all these techniques in a flexibly combined fashion appropriate to a particular stress or crisis situation. As always, the key to expertise and mastery is *practice, practice,* and *practice.*

PART II:

Pre-Incident
Mental Toughness Training

3

Arousal Control

The Nature and Purposes of Arousal

In common usage, the word *arousal* can have many meanings. We are aroused from a deep sleep or aroused to righteous anger by the injustice we see around us. Neurologists speak of levels of arousability to describe the clinical state of semicomatose patients. More commonly, as we go through our daily routines, we are more or less aroused by the events around us, depending on such things as the time of day, how stimulating or boring our present activity is, or whether or not the coffee machine is working.

In this chapter, the term *arousal* refers to the state of awareness and readiness for action that characterizes all conscious states. And like virtually all such states, arousal must be maintained at the appropriate level for a given task or situation in order for your activity to be adaptive for that task. Arousal can be thought of as existing on a continuum. The optimum state of arousal in any situation, whether routine or emergency, is that which energizes you for proper action but does not distract or impede you from carrying out the task.

For most active tasks, too little arousal results in flagging motivation, drifting attention, and a lackadaisical, inefficient approach to the task, like sitting through a boring classroom lecture and trying to catch what the instructor is droning on about. Too much arousal, on the other hand, sends you into adrenalin overdrive, and you become scattered, panicked, and again unable to complete the task effectively, like suddenly having the final exam thrown on your desk without preparation. Psychologists

43

will recognize this as the famous *Yerkes-Dodson law* or "in-verted-U" graph, where too little arousal bogs down task effi-ciency and too much derails it.

For the present discussion, arousal can be divided into two main types (Asken, 1993).

> *Primary arousal* flows from the performance demands of the situation itself, for example, a firearms qualifying exam on the shooting range. Here the officer must main-tain the right level of emotional energy to focus on his draw-aim-fire technique. Although officers will some-times speak of getting themselves "relaxed" before a match, they don't mean a dreamy, mellow state; what they're usually talking about is a sense of sharp, confi-dent focus, which involves a combination of proper arousal and attention (more on the latter in the next chapter). Thus, primary arousal provides the preparatory physical and mental readiness for, and focus on, the challenge at hand.

> *Secondary arousal* is extraneous and often unhelpful; it comes mainly from worrying, doubts, and concerns about how the officer will be evaluated—by superiors, peers, or his own self-scrutiny—and is thus closely con-nected with the concept of *performance anxiety* (Hays & Brown, 2004). It is this kind of secondary arousal that of-ficers try to minimize during training and evaluation ex-ercises and, as we'll soon see, during real-life police emergencies.

Another important variable influencing arousal level is *task complexity*. High arousal has less of a disruptive effect on sim-ple tasks than on complex ones. Actually, we know from the field of neuropsychology (Miller, 1988, 1990, 1993b) that there are three important variables that affect task performance, which can be remembered by the acronym, CNS, as in Central Nervous System, but in this case standing for Complexity, Nov-elty, and Speed.

Complexity refers to how many different elements of a task or situation you have to juggle at one time. For example, calming a distraught domestic assault victim is difficult enough, but will be far more challenging if there is also a drunk partner present who needs to be contained or arrested, and screaming children running around the house.

Novelty refers to how familiar or unfamiliar the task is. A skilled hostage negotiator may have handled hundreds of home, workplace, and bank robbery hostage calls, all with certain common elements, but if this particular call involves political terrorists who are making unusual demands, it will require far more concentration, focus, and outside information to handle effectively, precisely because there are so many novel features to the situation.

Speed refers to how quickly something must be done. All things being equal, tasks that have to be completed swiftly, such as directing traffic and pedestrians away from a potentially explosive chemical spill, will be more difficult than those in which the officer can take his time and deliberate over his actions, for example, waiting for hazmat to secure the scene before sorting out who did what to cause the tanker truck to roll over in the first place.

Optimum Arousal Level

The goal then, is to strive neither for a state of blissful repose nor wide-eyed hypervigilance, but to be able to induce an *optimum arousal level* (OAL) that is appropriate for a given task or situation. Some situations may require ramping up your arousal level to deal with the threat, while in other cases it may be necessary to calm yourself down so that extraneous arousal does not distract and disrupt your performance. Expert responders and peak performers in all fields seem to learn to control their level of arousal so that they can generate the necessary OAL for specific situations (Flin, 1996; Hays & Brown, 2004; Klein, 1996; Rodgers, 2006).

For example, a study of novice parachutists (Gal-Or et al, 1985) found that the best performance was seen in persons high in both anxiety and self-control, while the poorest performance was exhibited by persons with high anxiety and low self-control. Why? Apparently, being highly aroused can be either an asset or an impediment, depending on how well you can control it. Like any ability, some people have more innate talent in doing this than others, but for most of us, it is a skill that can be mastered with practice.

A related concept (Hannin, 2000) is the *individual zone of functioning* (IZOF), which seems to combine elements of arousal level and attentional control (discussed more fully in the next chapter). As typically described, the IZOF state involves a total focus on the present, an intentional direction of one's attention, and the ability to modulate emotion and arousal level that is appropriate to the task. This is an optimal mental state for a skilled task that is unique to each person.

Like any human state or trait, there is no one right OAL and IZOF for every individual (Hays & Brown, 2004). For one person, an ideal performance state might involve feeling relaxed, thrilled, and a bit apprehensive. Another person might perform best when angry, determined, or invigorated. Skilled performers in all fields appear to achieve their optimal pre-performance state in a way similar to athletes. They focus on the key factors of predictability, ritual, or routine, keeping the simple things simple so as to be able to allocate sufficient mental "disk space" to the novel features of the task at hand. How one interacts with others at the scene is one element of this mental resource management, and this will be discussed further below.

For the professional sniper, for example, many different mental tasks need to be carried out continuously, until the situation is resolved. One such sniper, who also happened to be a medic, described how important it was to keep his mind occupied and pull himself away a little bit, to "kind of stand outside of the emotional sphere" during an operation. Keeping unwanted emotions in check (at least till later) is a skill that depends in part on mastery of arousal (Hays & Brown, 2004),

Increasing Arousal

Students in my courses and seminars are often surprised that I introduce the topic of increasing arousal as part of the curriculum of stress management: "Aren't we supposed to be learning to relax?" But as explained above, it is just as important to be able to increase your arousal level when necessary as it is to reduce it: "Do you want to be all mellowed out for your forced entry of a crack house with armed suspects inside?" The key, then, is to be able to voluntarily induce, adjust, and maintain the OAL for that particular situation and to flexibly moderate it up or down as circumstances change. Some techniques for increasing arousal level range from the familiar to the unusual, and include the following (Asken, 1993; Hays & Brown, 2004).

Get Physical

Mental and physical arousal typically go together, and getting the blood pumping is a well-known method of psyching oneself up: just watch boxers, football players, performance artists, and even some public speakers prior to their event. Such *physical warm-ups* can consist of push-ups, jumping jacks, a jog around the track, and so on. This also has the added benefit of limbering up your body for physically demanding tasks to come. Just be careful not to prematurely exhaust yourself.

Listen to the Best

Another common psycher-upper is *music*. Everybody's got their favorite tunes, but pick a style of music that gets your heart thumping in a positive, enthusiastic way. Combining a rocking beat with physical exercise is a common method for jacking up your motivation and energy level. Just be careful not to let too much of a party atmosphere distract you from the seriousness of the operation you're about to undertake.

Pick Your Company

We commonly speak of emotions as being "contagious" and one of the most well-documented phenomena in social psychology (Salas et al, 1996) is the powerful effect that others' presence can have on our own mood and motivation. Indeed, physiological studies show that individuals who train and work together regularly attune their basic biorhythms with one another during high-stress activities that have been well-prepared for, whether it is a tight band performing in concert or a SWAT team mobilizing for a hostage rescue mission. The presence of others can thus have an enhancing or distracting effect, depending on the prevailing emotional climate. Therefore one's own proficiency at emotional self-regulation has repercussions for the whole team as well as the individual.

So, if you're gearing up for an important operation, you probably don't want to spend the immediately preceding period hanging out with a roomful of slugs and couch potatoes. *Selective association* (Asken, 1993) refers to spending time with others who are as excited and enthused as you are. It doesn't mean they have to be doing the same activity as you—they don't even need to be in the same room; for example, you can vicariously selectively associate with the players on a TV football or hockey team, if watching the game will give you the physical and mental pump you need.

There appear to be several components of this group association effect on individual performance (Bowers et al, 1996; Caplan & Killilea, 1976). One is *social support* where team members assist one another in emotional mastery, offer practical guidance in handling team tasks, and provide constructive feedback to enhance the team's overall performance. A related variable is *group cohesion,* which provides a mutual buffering function to the team members against potentially debilitating stress (Griffith, 1989). For example, a study of group cohesion in relation to command style in tank crews found that the best performance was exhibited by high-cohesive crews with leaders who were strong on "task and people orientation" (Tziner & Vardi, 1982).

Cue Yourself

Cues are prompts you give to yourself to influence your mental state—in this case, in the direction of increased arousal. *Cue words* to increase arousal can be general ("Win!" "Kick ass!") or specific to the person or situation ("First one in owns the room!"). These can be said out loud, muttered under one's breath, or just thought internally. *Cue sounds* ("Hoo-ah!") serve the same function, as do *cue images,* such as visualizing yourself controlling a crowd, apprehending a suspect, and so on (imagery and visualization will be discussed in greater detail in Chapter 5).

Pay Attention

As noted above, and as will be discussed further in Chapter 4, arousal and attention are interactive and can enhance or detract from each other. A practical implication of this is that your arousal level can be increased by using *attentional focus,* which involves bringing to bear all of your awareness and concentration on the task you need to perform and on the skills necessary to get the job done. This will be further elaborated in Chapter 4.

Promote Self-Efficacy

Self-efficacy statements involve telling yourself—again, either out loud or in your mind—that you can, indeed, carry out the task before you ("I can do it;" "Piece of cake"). These statements are often combined with cue words, sounds, or images for maximum effectiveness. In fact, many officers naturally utilize a combination of the above techniques when gearing up for a dangerous or challenging operation. This will be further described in Chapter 6.

Use Anger Productively

How many times have you been too tired or too lazy to do much of anything, and then somebody says something to get you riled, and suddenly you're bursting with righteous indignation. *Anger transformation* (Asken, 1993) involves thinking about something that makes you mad and gets your juices going. In essence, it's akin to "method acting" that Hollywood performers often use to psyche themselves into a role, and is also commonly used by athletes before a competition. Again, the guideline is situation-appropriateness. What you certainly want to avoid is your anger getting so out of control that it either becomes an emotional distraction from peak performance or leads to inappropriately forceful action that can end up getting you in trouble. A similar kind of *mental conditioning* technique will be discussed in Chapter 7.

Decreasing Arousal

This is usually the substance of most courses and programs in stress management and basically involves learning to control the physiology of arousal—to moderate the adrenalin rush that typically accompanies emergency situations. Again, this doesn't mean blissing-out: as noted earlier, most emergency situations can't be handled very effectively if the officer's mental state is akin to floating on a cloud. Still, there are many benefits to being able to calm one's own body and mind during a critical situation (Asken, 1993). Arousal control lowers anxiety and increases confidence during a call. A more relaxed state reduces the likelihood of impulsive action and resulting injury. A relatively relaxed, but assertively motivated state is conducive to learning new skills and to learning from one's mistakes on the spot: a kind of real-time 20/20 hindsight = 20/20 insight = 20/20 foresight application (Chapter 1).

Just remember that a state of physical and mental relaxation is not an all-or-none phenomenon. Many athletes, soldiers, and law enforcement officers, whose primary mental state on the job involves being continuously alert and vigilant, only understand relaxation from the perspective of a total letting down of one's guard, as during family vacations or a night at the pub with the guys. In their minds, "relaxation" may be equated with vulnerability and befuddlement. But one can be both relaxed and alert, in a state of calm determination that seems to characterize those who show stable and effective command leadership under fire (Flin, 1996; Miller, 2005b, 2006i).

It's kind of like the caffeine boost you get from a strong cup of coffee: alert, focused, and motivated, but not agitated or overly anxious. The more coffee you drink, however, the more that confidently pumped feeling turns to jitteriness and crankiness. There's a neurobiological reason for this: All stimulant substances (and the brain doesn't care if they're legal or not) increase the amount of *dopamine* in central nervous system, which is the high-motivation, "hey-I-can-do-it-let's-go" neurotransmitter. But with continued high stimulation over time, more and more of the dopamine becomes metabolized to *norepinephrine,* the more anxious, cautious, "hold-it-I'm-getting-a-bad-feeling-about-this" neurotransmitter. Eventually, even norepinephrine is depleted and the person just crashes into a state of fatigue or depression (Miller, 1988, 1990; Zuckerman, 1991). That's why it's important to be able to moderate your level of arousal, not just keep it on the highest setting all the time: you don't want to flame out prematurely.

Therefore, a particularly important role for relaxation and arousal control in law enforcement concerns calls in which there exists high personal danger over a relatively prolonged period of time, and where there is little the officer can do but bide his time and wait. These situations include being trapped in building and hoping for rescue, being a hostage during a prolonged negotiation, being pinned down by hostile fire and waiting for backup, and so on. Getting through such situations often requires that the officer be able to go into partial mental hibernation, to put his mental computer on standby mode, to keep the mental engine in neutral—pick whatever metaphor you like—to avoid expending precious energy, but at the same time being alert and aware enough to seize the initiative should the opportunity to do something constructive suddenly present itself.

Even if not in actual danger, prolonged law enforcement and emergency service operations are likely to involve long work shifts, alternating with briefer rest periods, such as in hostage negotiations, undercover operations, or mass casualty rescue operations (Miller, 1998d, 2005e, 2006j, in press-c). Most people find it difficult to go from high alert to standby at the drop of a hat. With the adrenalin still pumping, but physical, cognitive and emotional energy reserves depleted, the officer may find himself in a state of *agitated exhaustion*: too tired to function, too wired to rest. It is before getting to this point that the ability to consciously reduce your level of arousal can spell the difference between recharging your batteries and burning out your motor.

In this sense, the term *relaxation* denotes a flexible range of low-arousal techniques that can be utilized when the situation warrants. You train with many different kinds of weapons and equipment, knowing that you're going to become especially proficient and comfortable with only a small subset of these that you'll use in your daily routine police work. But it's nice to know you have some familiarity with the others if you ever need them. In the same way, in any given situation, you're probably never going to use all of the arousal control techniques described below—indeed, all of the skills and strategies in this book—but by practicing each of them, you'll come to learn which ones best suit your own temperament and psychophysiological response style, thus adding to your general stress management arsenal.

Relaxation Techniques

Learn to Relax

For more than half a century, the technique of *progressive muscle relaxation* has been the standard recipe of stress management and is by now so well-known that it will only be summarized here. The basic rationale is that much of what we experience as uncomfortably heightened arousal comes from feedback from tensed muscles and other bodily signals of arousal. Essentially, then, the progressive relaxation exercise focuses on one muscle group or body area at a time and guides the subject through an alternate tense-and-relax sequence until all major muscle groups are in a state of relative physiological quiescence. This is typically combined with slow, steady, diaphragmatic breathing (deep stomach breathing as opposed to shallow chest breathing) and one or more mental cuing or imagery techniques (see below) to further induce a state of psychophysiological calm.

Obviously, officers can't carry their lounge chairs to emergency calls or take time out from a burning building or gun battle to go through a tense-and-relax and breath-control protocol. Indeed, one of the features of effective, practical low-arousal techniques that make them useful in the field is the ability to utilize them quickly under adverse circumstances. Accordingly, the technique is first practiced in a peaceful, stress-free environment, such as in a psychologist's office or stress-management class, guided by the clinician's or instructor's soothing words or by the use of a commercially prepared or custom-made relaxation tape or CD.

Later, with continued practice in a variety of settings and conditions, the subject should be able to self-induce the relaxed state on his or her own, in his or her natural environment, without external prompting, and without having to go through the whole tense-and-relax sequence each time. For example, someone who finds himself tensing up in traffic might be able to quickly induce a more relaxed, yet alert, state while sitting behind the wheel.

Once the progressive relaxation technique has been practiced and mastered, many individuals are able to employ a kind of *instant relaxation*, or *conditioned relaxation* technique (Asken, 1993; Hays & Brown, 2004). By voluntarily reducing muscular tension, taking a calming breath, and using a cue word, the person is able to immediately lower physiological arousal and thereby induce a more calm and focused mental state. Like any highly trained technique, this becomes easier and more automatic with repeated practice.

Other low-arousal techniques utilize some components of the progressive relaxation protocol and add certain others.

Breath Deeply

Diaphragmatic breathing involves using the deep-breathing technique described above to trigger the entire relaxation response. This is often used along with a *cue word or phrase,* which may range from the spiritual ("God is with me;" "Om") to the mundane ("Chill;" "Okay, I'm good"), and is basically any word or phrase you've paired frequently with the full relaxation response and that you can now say to yourself to signal your body to relax. Similarly, a *cue image* is any mental scene you can invoke that has a calming effect, especially by virtue of having been paired with your initial relaxation response practice. Pick the modality or technique that works best for you: the key is to invoke some cue that enables you to quickly and voluntarily lower your arousal level to a degree that is appropriate for the situation you're in (Hays & Brown, 2004; Miller, 1994a; Olson, 1998).

Center Yourself

Centering (Asken, 1993) is a technique derived from Eastern meditation that involves combining diaphragmatic breathing with a *centering cue image*. Begin by taking a slow, deep diaphragmatic breath. On exhaling, slowly let your eyes close (or remain open if this is more comfortable for you) and focus your awareness on some internal or external point, such as your lower abdomen or an imaginary spot on the wall. Repeat this process until you feel yourself becoming calmer. This technique combines features of arousal control with attentional focusing, described further in Chapter 4.

Recently, centering has been applied to law enforcement training for arousal reduction in the field by Doss (2006, 2007). In this model, as soon as you feel yourself tensing or drifting toward negative thoughts, take a slow, deep breath from down in your abdomen. When you exhale, direct your attention to relaxing your muscles. Inhale deeply from the diaphragm and as you exhale silently, tell yourself to "relax" and "focus." As you say these words, let your muscles relax. Keep practicing until you can evoke this response at will.

Control Attention to Control Arousal

Centering is itself incorporated into a technique called *attention control training* or *attention management* (Asken, 1993; Hardy et al, 1996; Nideffer & Sharpe, 1978), which begins with inducing the centering response, and then presenting yourself with a task-relevant cue or instruction that focuses your attention on the immediate challenge at hand. This will be described further in Chapter 4.

Be Mindful

For some people, "trying to relax" is a contradiction in terms: the more they try to force themselves relax, the more tense they get. That's because, by definition, relaxation is something you have to learn to *let* happen, not *make* happen, and some individuals are just too challenged by the process to allow this to take place comfortably. In *mindfulness* training (Kabat-Zinn, 1994, 2003; Marra, 2005), the individual makes no conscious attempt to relax, but simply allows him- or herself to take in the sensations and images in the surrounding environment. Eventually, by taking the demand element out of the process, relaxation will usually occur as a beneficial "side effect." This kind of free-floating receptivity also underlies many of the attention-focusing strategies to be described in Chapter 4.

Use External Cues

Finally, just as *externally-based techniques* can be used to increase arousal, they can also be used to tone it down. These include music (calm instead of raucous) and selective association (spend your off hours at the beach or library instead of a hockey game or race track). Again, the more internal and external arousal control techniques you can use together, the greater will be the overall cumulative effect. Indeed, recent clinical research and practice have been moving away from an over-reliance on structured breathing and muscle relaxation techniques in favor of more naturalistic strategies (Huppert & Baker-Morissette, 2003; Marra, 2005; Miller, 1994a; Schmidt et al, 2000). Many of these will be described in the chapters to come.

4

Attention Control

The Nature and Purposes of Attention

With all the emphasis placed on controlling arousal and learning how to relax, it is easy to overlook the importance of being able to concentrate and focus attention in developing mental toughness skills for peak performance—a fact that is most glaringly obvious when things go wrong. To use one example, too narrow an attentional focus is often characterized as *tunnel vision,* which involves "missing the forest for the trees," that is, overfocusing on details while losing sight of the big picture. Conversely, trying to get a little of everything at once may result in *blurred vision*—here, the beam of attention is too broad, diffuse, and scattered to yield any useful information on how to respond. In emergency situations, one of the first mental faculties to be affected is the ability to control one's attention as required.

Attention is what allows you to focus on a situation or task so that sensory input is processed in a meaningful pattern. *Concentration* is the ability to consciously and purposefully direct and maintain your attention to a particular object or activity over time. By concentrating, you make a point to avoid distractions that could disrupt your performance. At the same time, it's important to be able to switch attention to another subject when necessary, and even maintain different types, levels, and targets of attention and concentration as needed at any given time. A third term, *awareness,* refers to the sum total of knowledge about your surroundings afforded by attention, concentration, and your sensory-perceptual faculties.

57

Effortful concentration, especially if prolonged, takes a great deal of mental energy and can be fatiguing. Accordingly, it is important to be able to produce a match between the often-changing demands of a critical situation and the precise level and direction of attention and concentration needed on a moment-to-moment basis. Some officers and emergency personnel do this automatically and instinctively; for most—like any other critical skill—it requires some degree of training and practice.

In fact, control of attention and concentration is so important that the brain has an entire neural network devoted to it, called the *reticular activating system* or RAS (Miller, 1990, 1993). This system consists of a complex pattern of neurons and fibers that connect the basic sensory modalities (vision, hearing, touch, pain, smell, taste, temperature, balance, and others) with the arousal, emotional, motivational, and thinking centers of the brain. In this way, what we experience through our senses is automatically coordinated with the proper response to that situation. Individuals who have suffered damage to the RAS may have eyes and ears that work fine, but the perceptions they take in have no significance to them; they are essentially unresponsive, even though the primary sensory pathways are intact. Thus, they may appear uninvolved with their surroundings, but they are not sleeping or in a coma—they don't respond because the sensory information that enters the nervous system just "doesn't register."

The closest any of us gets to this state in normal life is when we fail to hear someone right next to us talking in our ear because we're so focused on another person's conversation, riveted to a TV show, engrossed in a magazine article, or internally preoccupied with a troubling thought. An observer might say we're "distracted" or that our "mind is elsewhere." In fact, it may take an unexpected stimulus, such as a jabbing finger or a loud "Hellooooo . . ." to refocus our attention to the person trying to capture it. The neuropsychological bottom line is that we have a finite ability to focus attention on more than a few things at a time, whether on ourselves or in the environment. The key is to train the RAS and associated brain structures to do this more efficiently and controllably.

In fact, focus of attention may be one feature of *cognitive style* that varies among individuals and may be associated with certain personality traits (Miller, 1990; Shapiro, 1965). Research on this subject actually goes back to the 1950's when a team of psychologists (Gardner et al, 1959; Klein, 1954) carried out an extensive investigation of the personality profiles of a large group of psychiatric patients and healthy volunteers, and then compared the results of the personality assessment with those from a large battery of cognitive tests, measuring attention, concentration, memory, reasoning, spatial perception, and speed of mental processing.

This research revealed that there are huge differences in the way people experience, think, and act on reality. For example, some people's style of thinking involves a leveling-out of perceptions and memories, others a sharpening of focus on what they experience and remember. Some people can pick out the relevant features of a task and perform with great accuracy, but at a carefully slow and plodding speed. Others gleefully zip through the task, but make lots of clumsy errors. Some individuals tend to see similarities among things; others are more sensitive to differences. Some can use the power of logical analysis in a flexible way to deal with unexpected changes in routine; others get stuck in a rut or try to force the square peg of changing reality into the round hole of their old preconceptions.

What's more, this early study demonstrated that a person's cognitive style—the way they take in and process information—has a great deal to do with their basic personality. A person who tends to repress or gloss over unpleasant realities is typically aided by a broad, diffuse, "leveling" type of cognitive style that colors the world in broad strokes; the downside is that these individuals can often be scatter-brained to the point of irresponsibility. Conversely, the "sharpening" type of cognitive style goads the obsessive worry-wart to dwell and fuss over minutiae, often to the extent that the whole point of the activity is lost. Most of us are blends and permutations of the basic cognitive styles, which accounts for the myriad shades and colors of human personality (Miller, 1988, 1990, 2003a, 2003b, in press-f).

But back to attention: Like any human ability, mental or physical, some people may possess more of an innate talent for attentional control than others. But, again like most abilities, attentional control is a skill that can be learned, indeed, *must* be learned, for effective response in critical situations to take place because, in an emergency, a lapse or misfocus of attention and concentration can lead to costly mistakes. "I wasn't paying attention," "I missed the cue," "I wasn't thinking," "I had tunnel vision," "I dropped the ball," "I was too slow on the uptake," "I was somewhere else," "It got past me," are all phrases officers have used to describe lapses or disruptions of attention during critical calls.

Dimensions of Attention

A number of authorities (Asken, 1993; Doss, 2007; Hardy et al, 1996; Hays & Brown, 2004) have conceptualized the faculty of attention as lying along two interrelated dimensions: breadth of focus and direction of focus.

Breadth of Focus

Breadth of focus describes how narrow or wide the beam of attention is. When first encountering an unknown scene, officers typically don't want to overlook something important, so they set the attentional scan relatively wide to take in as much information as possible, much like using the wide angle lens setting of a surveillance camera. But if something critical is identified, then the focus narrows, like looking through a rifle sight to concentrate on the target and eliminate distractions. Here, all of your attention is riveted to the task at hand, at the calculated expense of losing information at the perceptual periphery; in other words, you're deliberately inducing tunnel vision, because that's what's needed right now for the specific task of acquiring a target and hitting it, either with a bullet or a camera click.

Ideal attention management entails the ability to focus on elements or "cues" that are relevant to performance while ignoring nonessential features. In fact, research has shown that the ability to manage attention in this fashion is one of the features distinguishing successful athletes from less successful players (Hays & Brown, 2004). Indeed, many situations require you to flexibly shift concentration from broad to narrow and back again, or even to maintain a kind of divided consciousness, focusing on a particular subject of interest while simultaneously keeping a portion of the attentional beam in a scanning mode so as not to overlook existing or emerging threats.

Direction of Focus

Another dimension is *direction of focus,* which can be internal or external. *External focus* is the most obvious, as it is important to be able to focus on the events taking place around you during the critical situation. But it may be just as important to *focus internally* on what is taking place mentally and physically within your own mind and body during the critical incident. This includes your own arousal level, balance, energy reserves, fear and anxiety, presence or threat of injury, or basic requirements like need for air or taking a bathroom break (Asken, 1993; Duran, 1999). Again, flexibility is the key, and during a critical incident, attention should monitor back and forth between internal and external, coordinating thought, feeling, and arousal with optimum task performance.

Training Attention

You've probably heard that if a person is blind, his or her other senses become much sharper. Actually, that's not quite true. What the blind person has learned to do is to make *maximum use* of his or her other senses in a way most of us don't have to. But each of us has the capacity to sharpen *all* of our senses and we don't have to lose a sensory modality to do it. As noted earlier, controlling the sharpness and power of your senses has a lot to do with learning to control your brain's RAS-attentional system.

Being able to flexibly control attention requires that you master three fundamental dimensions of attention and concentration (Asken, 1993): (1) *Intensity* = being able to concentrate *hard* enough; (2) *duration* = being able to concentrate *long* enough; and (3) *flexibility* = being able to *shift* concentration when necessary.

Mastering these three dimensions involves practicing what Asken (1993) calls the *attention-fixation-generalization technique,* which has also recently been described by Doss (2007), and which I have adapted for use in my law enforcement courses and training seminars. For this technique, think of attention as a type of flashlight beam with a constant wattage but with a variable aperture. This allows you to broaden the beam to a soft glow that dimly but fully illuminates the whole room, or narrow it down to a single, thin, bright shaft of light that creates a tiny but blazing spot on the wall. Another analogy is to an adjustable garden hose nozzle that allows you to cover a wide swath of lawn with a broad, misty spray or zero in on a single shrub with a fast, concentrated water jet. Beam or stream—pick whatever metaphor that best helps you grasp the concept and master the methodology.

Also bear in mind that you probably won't become a proficient exponent of all the following steps in one or two sessions. Like any other skill, keep practicing these techniques, sequentially and concurrently, until you achieve your desired level of proficiency.

To begin training in this technique, first assume a relatively comfortable position, relatively free of distractions. Eventually, you should be able to evoke and utilize this technique even under conditions of extreme stress and chaos but, at first, practice it in a relatively quiet setting.

Pick an object in the room—a picture, a lamp, a cup, even a spot on the wall—and visually focus your attention on it as intently and as long as possible. Try to keep all of your attention on this object, tuning out any other stimuli in the room. Hold that focus for as long as possible. Then, voluntarily shift your attention away from the object to another object in the room. Make that your focus of attention. Try this with a few other objects around the room.

Now, try it with sounds. Focus on a lawnmower in a neighbor's yard, a TV character mumbling in the next room, or the hum of the fridge. Pick one sound source and hone in on it.

Now, switch to another sound, and then another, as you did with the visual objects. Keep doing this until it starts to feel natural.

Now, try going back and forth between visual and auditory stimuli. To make it interesting, try it with different objects (switch from a visual image of the couch to the sound of the fridge) or with the same object (swing your attention back and forth from the TV picture to the sound). Remember to take your time initially and not try to rush things: keep practicing and you'll get it.

Now, broaden the beam. Scan the entire room and become aware of as many sources of stimuli as possible: the objects in the room, their shapes, colors, textures, and proximity to one another, the drone of the air conditioner or people talking, any street noise coming in from outside, any smells or temperature changes, the level of illumination in different parts of the room, the pressure of the seat on your legs and tush, the feel of your clothes on your skin.

Pay attention to internal sources of physical and mental stimulation, as well: Are you hot or cold, hungry or thirsty? Are you comfortable in your seat? Do you have to use the bathroom? Tired or rested, calm or nervous, happy or sad, interested or bored?

You may find it overwhelming at first to try to attend to so many features of your internal and/or external environments at once. You'll probably lose your focus on one thing as you try to concentrate on another, like trying to follow several simultaneous conversations around the dinner table. As the attentional beam gets stretched more and more broadly, you may find it thinning out to the point that you're not really paying attention to anything in particular—the mental flashlight flickers, the garden hose sputters.

Take heart. This scanning ability will improve with practice, and will further improve as you learn to also control the *intensity* of the scanning beam. For now, however, pull in the beam-width a little bit to the point where you're able to focus on as many things as possible, while keeping those percepts reasonably within your span of attention.

Next, keep maintaining multiple foci of attention but start varying the intensity and beam-width of each. Now, you'll actually have several beams of attention branching out simulta-neously. Some will be narrowly and intensely focused on one feature of the environment, such as a person talking to you or a scene played out on the TV. Others will be more broadly scan-ning the environment, taking in such things as the number of people in the room, the layout of the furniture, points of access and exit, and so on.

In reality, you already do this in your daily life. Think about having a conversation with a passenger while driving: you're usually so tuned in to what you're gabbing about with the other person that you're virtually unconscious of the driving process itself; you only pay special attention to the road if some unex-pected event occurs, like the car in front of you suddenly brak-ing. While this kind of divided consciousness could prove dangerous, it's impressive how often accidents *don't* happen be-cause, for most of us, the driving process is such a well-prac-ticed, overlearned skill, that we can allocate our RAS resources elsewhere.

Ideally, in a real-life police emergency, your intense, narrow attentional beam might be focused on a criminal making a threatening gesture toward you, with other beams more broadly and less intently scanning important peripheral and internal features of the environment: being alert for sounds of footsteps behind you, avenues of escape around the room, your own heartbeat and respiration rate, the smell of gunpowder or drug residue, and so on. It is in just these kinds of critical situations that the ability to flexibly allocate attention in many directions, in response to changing circumstances, might save your life (Doss, 2006, 2007; Garner, 2005; Garner & Doss, 2005). This will be further explored in Chapter 11.

Another practical example involves officer-involved shoot-ings, in which officers typically describe a sense of tunnel-vi-sion during the episode. In retrospect, many report that they were so focused on the suspect's gun or their own actions that they completely tuned out anything else that was going on; as a consequence, they have difficulty remembering what transpired during the event. This is probably because all the environmen-tal stimuli that were shut out of the brain's perceptual channels by an over-focused RAS during the emergency never got the chance to be recorded accurately by the brain's memory system. This will be discussed more fully in Chapter 12.

In my law enforcement courses and seminars, I ask each officer to recount a personal critical incident from his or her own career and describe the thoughts, feelings, and actions that accompanied it. Then, as a class, we run through some practice sessions of the attention-fixation-generalization technique described above. After that, I ask each officer to re-create the original incident in his or her own mind and imagine how it might have been different if they had used the technique they just learned. Finally, I encourage the officers to practice the technique in their daily patrol activities until it becomes natural and automatic, so they'll be ready to employ it in the event of an emergency.

As always, the goal of learning any skill is for it to become so ingrained and natural that you're hardly aware that you're using it. This can only be achieved through practice and application in as wide a variety of settings as possible, i.e. ITTS.

5

Utilizing Imagery

The ability to use imagery to mentally project oneself into a different mindset or state of being is a time-honored psychological technique for improving skills in sports and the performing arts (Hays & Brown, 2004), and only quite recently has this skill begun to be specifically applied to law enforcement training (Doss, 2006, 2007).

Multisensory Imagery

Imagery training is sometimes referred to as *visualization* training (Olson, 1998), but I agree with Asken (1993) and Hays & Brown (2004) that *imagery* is the preferable term because—as with attention control discussed in the last chapter—such training ideally should involve sensory images in all modalities, not just vision. Like any skill, the use of effective imagery requires practice, general at first, but ultimately focused on the type of imagery that most closely replicates the actual situation that the performer will be in.

As with all these techniques, this presupposes adequate training and experience with the skill itself as a prerequisite to imaging yourself doing it. You can spend all day imaging yourself playing a killer lead guitar solo or competing in a Nascar race but, if you've never actually *done* these things, then you might as well image yourself flying like Superman. Imagery, then, is a technique to enhance performance of a skill, once that skill has been fundamentally learned and mastered in real life. That is, imagery is not the same as fantasy. It does not take the place of hard work in the real world, but may improve it in proportion to how much the real-life skill improves (Duran, 1999; Hays & Brown, 2005). To be effective, the image must be as accurate as possible.

Note that I'm using "image" as a verb. That's because the term, "imagine" typically connotes fantasy and daydreaming ("Imagine yourself on a sandy beach . . ."), while the imagery exercises described in this chapter are grounded in reality—the reality of whatever down-to-earth law enforcement critical tasks you may have to face on the job. As long as we've got our dictionaries open, I might also point out that the term, "daydreaming" does in fact incorporate the powerful use of imagery, often with just the type of rapt absorption and concentration we were trying to encourage in the last chapter.

However, the difference is that, in daydreaming, the dream leads the dreamer: what makes the process so enjoyable is that there's relatively little conscious effort involved; that is, we passively experience the story as it unfolds in our own mind. But the kind of imagery we're going to discuss in this chapter requires a precise kind of focused, effortful, volitional guidance because you're training it for a specific purpose: to hone and refine your response skills to critical situations.

Finally, we appeal to precedent: "to image" tends to be used this descriptive way in the sports psychology literature, so retaining this usage is just being consistent with a larger body of work.

Uses of Imagery

There are several important uses of effective imagery for enhancing the performance of law enforcement and emergency services personnel (Asken, 1993).

Simulate Training Scenarios

A basic use of imagery is for *situation simulation,* which is an important component of all uses of imagery. You can't train in every situation every time you want to, but you can learn to evoke the scenarios mentally. Combined with actual practice in real-life and realistic-simulation settings (obstacle track, firing range), this mental drilling can integrate with real-life drilling for enhanced performance.

Enhance Real-World Skills

Successful simulation leads directly to the use of imagery for *skill enhancement,* in which the imagery is used to mentally rehearse a particular physical activity. For example, you might image yourself conducting a crime scene search or accurately drawing down on a difficult target with your weapon (see Chapter 12). You might start imaging subsets or subsequences of the entire activity, then stringing them together until you can mentally simulate the entire skill from start to finish (Duran, 1999).

Analyze and Correct Errors

In using imagery for *error analysis and correction,* the officer engages in a kind of internal operational debriefing, mentally "replaying the tape" of a recent real-life incident, recalling as many details as possible, and utilizing the 20/20/20 hindsight/ insight/foresight principle to self-correct any errors or misjudgments that were made.

This technique can be effectively combined with real-life operational debriefing data from outside sources, so that you can include this factual information in your mental operational critique. Note that, to varying extents, many officers do this spontaneously after a difficult call. The key is to master the use of this kind of imagery so that accurate details can be recalled during the hindsight review and appropriate corrections can be made during foresight mental rehearsal. This prevents an internal operational review from degenerating into an emotionally disruptive self-flagellation session that has little practical benefit.

Mentally Prepare for Action

Imagery can also be used proactively at the front end of an anticipated critical operation, for *response preparation.* In addition to regular mental drills for possible future events, imagery for response preparation can actually be used on-scene, in the immediate preparatory phase of an operation, such as a narcotics raid or SWAT team tactical assault. For example, officers can image themselves moving in, securing the scene and making arrests. Again, it's important that these internal scenarios be as realistic as possible, not simply wishful-thinking fantasies—that is, not daydreams. Many officers instinctively use these kinds of psyching-up imagery techniques before a complex or difficult operation.

Enhance Confidence

Finally, imagery can be used for *confidence enhancement.* Recalling past successes and utilizing multimodal imagery of the sensory, emotional, and visceral exhilaration of completing a task well done can enhance the feelings of competence and confidence. This can also be used as part of response preparation noted above. And both of these techniques interplay with arousal regulation, discussed in Chapter 3.

For example, *coping images,* in which the performer mentally constructs a difficult scene and then develops methods for handling the situation, may be used as an active aspect of contingency planning. Hays & Brown (2004) describe how one officer who straddled the roles of both sniper and medic, was able to use imagery along with relaxed breathing to mentally rehearse how he would respond to traumatic situations.

Visual-Motor Behavior Rehearsal

Developed by Suinn and colleagues (1972, 1984, 1985) in the domain of sports psychology and adapted by Asken (1993) to the needs of emergency service workers, *visual-motor behavior rehearsal* (VMBR) combines the relaxation response (Chapter 3) with multisensory imagery to mentally rehearse and enhance skills for peak performance. It is an extension of mental imagery, in that it combines the psychological aspect of generating the mental image with feedback from the performance of a physical skill (Lane, 1980). This method has been used successfully for enhancing skill in a number of sports, including karate, basketball, racquetball, tennis, golf, diving, gymnastics, cross-country running, and track and field (Behncke, 2006).

As typically practiced, VMBR involves three phases:

First, *inducing an appropriate arousal level* provides the psychophysiological background state that will be most conducive to the proper mental imagery, which involves combining the skills of this chapter with those of Chapter 3.

Second, *visualizing performance through various imagery techniques* allows the kind of internal rehearsal described in this chapter.

Third, *performing the actual skill under realistic conditions* (i.e., ITTS) reinforces the training link between the imagery exercises and the real-life skill.

A particularly useful application of VMBR is to employ the imagery of the task at the same time as you're doing the task itself. Repeating this process with the target skill during training reinforces the feedback connection between the mental imagery exercise and the actual performance. In that way, adjustments in both the real-life skill and the imagery process can be maintained in parallel and in real-time. Thus, the rationale behind VMBR is to keep mental imagery and skill performance closely associated in training, which should result in an enhancement of overall performance because the individual can fine-tune both processes simultaneously (Lane, 1980; Behncke, 2006).

How to Use VMBR

To utilize VMBR, first employ one of the exercises for inducing the relaxation response described in Chapter 3. This will allow you to get into a state of emotional calmness and clarity that will promote the ability to focus and evoke a complete simulation of the imagined scenario. Now, pick a situation that you have trained for and experienced in real life. Mentally walk yourself through the scene in real-time, evoking as many sensory and experiential details as possible.

For an error-correction exercise, mentally replay yourself doing exactly what you recall having done during the actual event. Then, mentally rewind the tape and image yourself performing the way you would, now that you have additional data and insight (the 20/20/20 rule). Rewind to the beginning of the incident and image yourself mentally preparing for it. Fast-forward and image yourself feeling competent and confident after successfully completing the task. Then, splice the parts together and mentally play the scenario in real-time sequence as many times as necessary until it feels natural and unforced.

VMBR with Police Officers

Although Asken (1993) has extensively utilized this technique with firefighters and emergency service workers, I was able to locate only one study that empirically evaluated the effectiveness of VMBR specifically for skill enhancement of police recruits. Shipley & Baranski (2002) randomly assigned 54 members of the Ontario Provincial Police Force training program to either a VMBR treatment or a non-treatment group prior to undergoing a highly stressful live-fire exercise. Results showed no differences between the VMBR group and the control group in the physical manifestations of anxiety (blood pressure, heart rate, perspiration, muscle tension, breathing rate) or in overall self-confidence, but the VMBR subjects did show lower levels of cognitive anxiety (i.e. their thought processes were clearer, less negative, and less distractible), and—most importantly—they showed better actual performance on the critical event scenario; that is, they achieved significantly higher scores on "assailant hits" during the live-fire exercise.

What is especially intriguing and encouraging about these findings is that they do not oversell VMBR (and, by implication, other mental training techniques) as a magical solution or miracle cure. Indeed, the VMBR subjects felt just as much somatic anxiety (heart thumping, palms sweating) as the control group, yet they were able to cognitively keep it together more effectively in order to focus on the task at hand. Additionally, even though the training group did not report feeling more confident than the control group, when it came to real-world performance—number of hits on the live-fire target range—they performed significantly better.

Thus, one of the strengths of mental training techniques is precisely that they are not all-or-nothing: even if you're feeling nervous and unsure, you may still show peak performance by focusing on the job that needs to be done, tuning out distractions, and letting your training click in. That is, while confidence certainly helps, just because you're not strutting around with a cocky "bring-em'-on" attitude before an operation, doesn't mean you won't perform effectively. Remember, this study did not specifically incorporate self-confidence imagery; it would be interesting to do a follow-up study to see if that variable could be positively affected as well.

For now, the take-away message is: Utilize all of the METTLE techniques, including imagery, to reinforce the 20/20/20 rule and the ITTS principle, not to substitute for them. For any skill worth learning, there is no shortcut to training and practice.

6

Using Thought and Language

In the last chapter, we saw how imagery can be invoked and utilized for enhancing skill development in a variety of domains. But human beings are unique among creatures precisely because we can think and transmit our thoughts in the form of spoken and written language. We can communicate our ideas and emotions to others and, just as importantly, we can articulate our thoughts and feelings to ourselves. Thinking and language are recursive and mutually reinforcing: our words express what we want to convey and, in the telling, often reinforce the very thoughts and feelings that gave rise to them.

The upside is that rational thought and language are what make our whole civilization possible. The downside is that we can just as easily think and talk ourselves into delusion and despair. Indeed, natural variations in the use of thought and language comprise further elements of cognitive style and personality that distinguish individuals from one another (Miller, 1990, 2003a, 2003b). The goal of this chapter is to teach you how to use thought and language productively, as tools of your mental toughness training program.

Thought Stopping

Sometimes, the best thing you can do with a dysfunctional thought or distressing internal dialog is to interdict it and banish it from consciousness. Everyone has had the experience of "talking myself into trouble," and there is ample evidence from both practical experience and empirical research that negative, self-defeating statements and thoughts have a deleterious effect on skilled performance (Hardy et al, 1996). Being able to stop non-productive thoughts and develop an internal dialog containing positive countermeasures to negative thoughts has been repeatedly demonstrated to improve performance (Van Raalte & Brewer, 2002).

Thought stopping is not as strange or diabolical as it sounds, and in fact is only a systematic application of something we all do when we need to keep unproductive ruminating thoughts from clogging our cognitive channels. During an emergency call, the combination of high internal arousal and high external distraction may propel cycling loops of negative thoughts and images that prevent you from making important decisions and critical judgment calls. Think of thought stopping as the Ctrl+Alt+Del sequence of your cognitive keyboard that can clear your mental screen when it freezes up. Thought stopping can also be used prior to a critical incident to keep negative ruminations from sapping your motivation and determination, or be used following the incident to prevent pointless, unproductive second-guessing or self-criticism that may impair your performance on the next call and keep you from utilizing the more productive 20/20/20 hindsight/insight/foresight review process.

Thought stopping is not an instant cure-all for negativity in general and it is not an excuse for failing to confront real-life problems that require more long-term solutions. It is not self-deception or self-delusion. In fact, if maladaptive repression and denial are a chronic pattern for you, you'll eventually need to resolve the circumstances and mind-sets that generate the negative thoughts and dysfunctional behaviors in the first place. But the thick of a critical incident is not a time to deal with issues, it's a time for rapid, effective action. If untreated diabetes makes you more prone to cardiovascular injury, you can deal with your blood glucose levels and insulin dosages at the next visit to your endocrinologist; but if you're lying in the street bleeding after a car wreck, the paramedic is only interested in keeping you alive long enough so that you can manage the underlying condition later. For now, the priority is to survive. So it is with mental emergencies: first, stay safe and complete the mission; then deal with the background issues when you can.

Utilizing Thought Stopping

Thought stopping can be combined with imagery (Chapter 5) to clear the mind and enhance performance (Asken 1993).

The first step is to monitor your consciousness for the presence of negative thoughts. Usually, finding these little demons will be the least of your problems, since they may be screaming louder than anything else in your head.

To halt a negative thought, forcefully tell yourself "No!" or "Stop!" Or visualize a flashing STOP sign or neon slash-in-circle symbol. Be as creative as you want to be and utilize whatever phrase or image works best for you (many of the examples cited by the officers in my courses are unprintable). Say them aloud if necessary, of course being mindful of the sensibilities of others around you, or say them to yourself. If a word or image doesn't do it for you, try some other stimulus: a sharp breath, a pinch on your arm, a riff or lyric from a favorite song—basically, any cue you can give yourself that will be jarring enough to abort the negative thought.

But, like nature, the human mind abhors a vacuum, so the best way to keep the negative thought from sneaking or barging back in is to insert something into your consciousness to take its place, something that is diametrically opposed to, and incompatible with, the negative thought. This would be the place to insert a confidence-building affirmation, positive mental image, or instructional cue (see below). Then, actually perform the activity to the best of your ability so that your constructive actions occupy your mind and your real-world success becomes the basis for future positive thoughts (20/20/20 and ITTS).

Cognitive Restructuring

This mechanical-sounding mental technique actually helps you do the opposite: break out of certain rigid thinking traps that jam your cognitive gears and help you utilize more flexible decision-making and problem-solving strategies in stressful circumstances. In *cognitive restructuring,* you are using your *metacognition,* or "observing ego," to make a command decision about what thoughts you will permit to dominate your thinking before, during, and after the critical event. Cognitive restructuring is aimed at unjamming and re-tuning certain automatic thoughts or cognitive distortions that we build up out of habit, and that get in the way of clear, adaptive thinking.

There are several types of automatic thoughts that can plague law enforcement and emergency service workers, with various solutions for dealing with them (Asken, 1993).

All-Or-Nothing Thinking

In *all-or-nothing thinking,* things are either black or white, never shades of gray. The most common expression of this in law enforcement work is the attitude that if I didn't do everything perfectly, the whole operation was a screw-up: "If I'd seen the knife in his hand a second earlier, he wouldn't have had time to stab that kid." "If I hadn't made that comment on the phone, he would've let all the hostages go." "If we don't bust all the dealers in this ring, the undercover operation will be a failure." Because human nature is normally risk-averse, we tend to pay more attention to negatives than to positives, which is okay when the goal is to operationally debrief ourselves so that our performance is better next time; indeed, this is encouraged as part of the 20/20/20 process. But focusing on negatives as if the positives didn't even exist serves only to drain energy and sap motivation—it is counterproductive to future performance.

To counteract all-or-nothing thinking, remind yourself that you are absolutely responsible for what you can control, but not what you can't. Another way of putting this is that you are responsible for your *efforts,* not the *outcome.* Now, of course, your efforts influence the outcome and it's your responsibility to ensure you have the proper talent, skill, training, and practical experience for a particular operation. But if you can honestly tell yourself (or have someone else more objectively tell you) that you did everything you realistically could, but some or all aspects of the call turned bad due to circumstances beyond your perception or control, then go ahead and feel bad about what happened, but don't unnecessarily *blame* yourself. Success is never guaranteed, and carrying around excess tons of unwarranted martyrdom can only slow you down the next time.

Overgeneralization

In *overgeneralization,* we take one example of something and apply it to all future situations. Or we pick one characteristic of a person—ourselves or others—and make that the sole defining feature of the person, excluding or minimizing everything else (trial lawyers and cognitive psychologists will recognize this as the *fundamental attribution error).* Once we've pigeonholed the person or situation, we then interpret everything about them in terms of this first impression. If that sounds a lot like the definition of *prejudice,* it's because prejudice almost always involves some degree of overgeneralization ("Those people are all . . ."). And it's sometimes too easy to prejudice ourselves against ourselves when we feel we're somehow not measuring up to our own standards.

The keywords of overgeneralization are *always* and *never:* "Domestic assault calls always turn out bad." "I never seem to say the right thing when I'm mediating a citizen dispute on my patrol." To counteract overgeneralization, actively seek out exceptions to the supposed rule and focus on them: "Well, there was this domestic call where I was really able to connect with the husband because it turns out we both came from the same small town, and then I was able to talk him down."

Disqualifying the Positive

A related cognitive distortion is *disqualifying the positive:* "Okay, so I was able to talk down the guy from my home town, but how many calls are going to have that kind of lucky coincidence? I'm still lousy at communication." You can counteract this in two main ways. One is to remind yourself that you still had to communicate with the guy; your common geographical origin didn't solve the problem all by itself. So maybe you can learn to generalize these talk skills to the next situation where your background is different from the citizen's. The second strategy is to recall task-relevant information: remember your training, do your best job, and expect a positive outcome. If you're really using your skills correctly, this is not wishful thinking, but a realistic bumping up of the odds.

Positive Affirmations

Related to the subject of confidence-enhancement is the technique of using *affirmations* (Asken, 1993). Basically, these are positive statements we make to ourselves about ourselves, referencing our own abilities. They are not narcissistic self-inflations or empty boasts; on the contrary, to be effective, what is being affirmed has to be based on genuine, real-life competencies that have been worked for and earned. Otherwise, such empty affirmations can quickly approach "Saturday Night Live"-like levels of parody. But sometimes, when we're under critical stress, or have just been pummeled by a series of downturns, we may forget that we still have positive qualities and competencies we can be proud of. And if no one is there to remind us, we have to be able to remind ourselves, lest our brooding turn to despair and further degrade our performance.

Types of Affirmations

Although these are hardly rigid categories and frequently overlap, Asken (1993) divides affirmations into three main groups.

> *Personal affirmations* are general self-statements that recognize your positive qualities as a human being: "I'm a stand-up guy." "I'm a smart gal." "My family knows I'd do anything for them." "I'm in great shape; I really take care of my health." "There are people out there who really love me."

> *Professional affirmations* are self-statements that recognize the positive aspects of your work in law enforcement: "The citizens in my patrol area respect me because

they know I'm fair, but that I won't take crap." "I've earned every promotion honestly and I deserve every bit of credit." "I'm the go-to guy in the department when anybody needs advice about weapons and tactics."

Performance affirmations are self-statements that recognize positive aspects of your skills or performance as they relate to a specific incident or operation: "Nobody was able to make sense of that crime scene till I came along." "Those hostages would've been toast if I hadn't talked the bad guy down." "I think fast, I speak well, and that's why that couple didn't end up bashing each other and hurting the kids."

Using Affirmations

It often helps to compose a realistic list of the positive qualities you can feel proud of. Again, you needn't—indeed, shouldn't—go around waving this list in your colleagues' faces, unless you enjoy being the object of scorn and ridicule. No one needs to know about the list, except you. In fact, it can be a strictly mental list, as long as you can recall the items when you need them. The objective is to have a ready set of positive qualities about yourself that you can invoke when you start to feel dejected and demoralized.

Asken (1993) delineates a number of principles to guide the use of positive affirmations. None of these is written in stone, and if you have a more comfortable way of expressing these affirmations, go ahead. That is, think of the following as flexible guidelines, not strict directives.

Practice makes perfect. Keep affirmations handy but don't overdo them to the point where they become meaningless, parroted repetitions.

Be positive. Not: "My record-keeping could be better, but at least I'm no slouch on the range," But: "I'm a damned good marksman, and if I put my mind to it, I can bring my paperwork up to speed."

It's all about "I." Not: "A lot of people seem to appreciate my investigative skills," But: "I'm the top crime scene analyst in the department."

Stay in the present. Not: "I've been a great patrol cop," or, "I'll try to improve my people skills," But: "I know how to talk to citizens to keep trouble from escalating on my beat."

Be honest with yourself. To put it bluntly, a positive self-statement can't help if, deep down, you know that it's bullshit.

Don't mistake the sizzle for the steak. Remember that affirmations do not replace skills and training. Actually, none of the stress-management and motivational techniques described in this chapter—or in this book—are intended to substitute for skills and training, but to enhance them, i.e. ITTS.

Don't set up unrealistic expectations. Affirmations are different from self-coaching or motivational self-talk (see below), which are aspirational encouragements for future performance. Affirmations, as discussed here, are positive confidence-bolstering statements that are based on skills and accomplishments that have already been earned and recognized. Consistent with the truth-and-reality guidelines above, if the affirmations aren't real, they won't stick.

Task-Relevant Instructional Self-Talk

When you first learn a skill during training, it's common to have your instructor talk you through the steps. For example, learning to use the equipment in a patrol car or mastering proper firing patterns on the range typically require that you first be shown how to do the task, then do it with explicit verbal guidance from the trainer, then only with a few cues, then maybe with the instructor just observing and making a few comments afterward, and finally doing it all by yourself.

Under conditions of stress, automaticity of performance of even well-trained skills often breaks down, and the smooth flow of the activity can be disrupted by distraction, confusion, and high emotion (Doss, 2006; Hays & Brown, 2004; Regehr & Bohrer, 2004). Athletes, musicians, stage actors, public speakers, soldiers, ER doctors, politicians, and police officers all speak of "choking under pressure." Worse, negative self-statements tend to become increasingly pessimistic and self-deprecatory, ranging from a simple "Oh, shit" to a run-on, self-deprecatory harangue: "This is going bad, we'll never make it through this one. What an idiot—I thought I could do this, but I can't. How do I get myself into these hopeless situations . . . ?"

At these times, it can be very useful to invoke an internalized representation of your teacher or mentor mentally talking you through a skill or procedure. As with a number of this book's strategies, many officers do this automatically and instinctively during stressful operations. Asken (1993) makes this process explicit in describing what he calls *task-relevant instructional self-talk* (TRIST), which involves using clear, succinct, short phrases by which you instruct yourself to execute your skills. This is not the same as using motivational self-statements, which were discussed above, although they may be especially useful when used in combination. In TRIST, you mentally put your instructor on your shoulder—or become your own instructor—to guide you through the nuts and bolts of the skill or activity. Accordingly, in TRIST, your self-talk focuses on the response-enhancing, task-relevant technical instructions on how to carry out the task itself.

Employing TRIST During a Critical Incident

Although the focus of TRIST is mainly cognitive and instructional, there are a number of arousal-regulating and emotion-modulating components, gleaned from some of the techniques discussed in previous chapters, that set the stage for the proficient application of TRIST.

The first step is to relax, or at least lower your arousal sufficiently so you can focus on the self-instruction you're about to give yourself—or, for that matter, focus on anything else that's relevant to the situation at hand. In discussing applications of self-talk to law enforcement training, Doss (2006) points out that, before initiating or changing one's self-talk, it is necessary to take a step back and become aware of what is being said and what needs to be said. Positive and negative thoughts are often mixed ("I've handled this kind of emergency fine before, but the present mess looks like it's out of control"). In these circumstances, it is necessary to identify both beneficial thoughts and harmful thoughts because you don't want to throw out the good with the bad. Once you've made this differentiation, it is then important to make a conscious effort to purposely include those thoughts that seem to help performance and banish those that impede it.

Next, use positive self-statements and confidence-building affirmations and imagery to bolster yourself: "I'm doing fine; this is just a tough call. I'm going to get my bearings and nail this thing." Note that this is not to encourage unrealistic overconfidence or dangerous foolhardiness: if the situation really *is* hopeless, then use your wits and training to get the hell out of there. Also remember that both optimism and pessimism can be contagious, so if realistic and feasible, encourage a positive attitude in others around you as well. As everybody's confidence increases, this will raise the morale and motivation of the whole team, increasing the chances of a successful operation. Once again, however, the optimism must be realistic to avoid your team becoming a herd of lemmings marching off a cliff.

Now, focus on the skill or technique you need to handle the call. For the immediate task at hand, try to forget about the outcome and consequences, and focus on the process and execution of the skill. If it helps, put your instructor on your shoulder and speak through his or her voice. Express the instruction in relatively short, task-relevant phrases and as positive statements: "Scan and clear the room; okay, level 1, level 2, level 3—clear." You can try combining the instructional talk with instructional imagery (Chapter 5), picturing yourself doing the task correctly, but use this only if it helps, not if it distracts you from the task at hand.

Remember that skill-focused TRIST is not the same as using motivational affirmations, but you may want to intersperse the latter with the former to bolster overall confidence during the operation: "Check unidentified objects or packages—hey, I was the top guy in the bomb squad course." Again, almost all of the mental toughening and performance enhancement techniques work best when used in creatively individualized combinations.

7

Psychological Survival Training

Life and Death in Police Work

Although most cops on any given day won't experience a critical incident or life-and-death encounter, when these incidents do happen, they always seem to come down fast and hard. Indeed, noted law enforcement expert John Violanti (1999) refers to the "civilian combat" that characterizes many aspects of law enforcement work. The US Department of Justice reports that, in the decade 1994–2003, over 571,000 officers were assaulted during confrontations (Burns, 2006).

Doss (2006, 2007) points out that one of the most stressful and demoralizing things law enforcement officers can experience on the job is the feeling that they are losing a fight with a suspect. Nothing will induce panic faster than an officer, realizing that what he thought was his best move, has just been countered by his opponent.

Consistent with the present book's approach, Doss (2006, 2007) emphasizes the importance of thoughts experienced during combat and the fact that these thoughts are powerfully influenced by the officer's attitude toward his opponent and his conceptualization of his own strengths and abilities. How the officer will respond to the emotions induced by a life-and-death struggle depends on four primary factors: (1) the officer's individual personality; (2) his level of either natural or learned emotional control; (3) how he reacts to those emotions; and (4) his level of emotional flexibility. As noted in previous chapters, key in controlling emotions is controlling the thoughts that can give rise to them.

Doss (2006, 2007) points out that, in most conflicts, whether fistfights, gun battles, or even critical verbal confrontations such as hostage negotiations, it is not necessarily the individual who has perfect textbook performance who wins, but the combatant who makes the fewest mistakes and rebounds most quickly from the mistakes that do occur—skills and competencies that rely on the principles of satisficing and RPDM discussed in Chapter 2. That's why it's critical that officers equip themselves not just with defensive gear and tactical fighting skills but also with *psychological body armor*: the methods and techniques for dispelling distractions, refocusing concentration, and maintaining emotional control and confidence during life-and-death critical incidents.

Surviving Life and Death Encounters

Here is where many of the psychological training techniques discussed in the previous chapters come together to enhance survival in the most extreme police emergencies, when your life is literally on the line. In his work with police officers, Blum (2000) has noted that, all other things being equal, a crucial factor that frequently makes the difference between whether an officer survives or succumbs to a deadly encounter is something he calls *positive mental attitude,* which seems to be a general term for the iron will to survive. Garner (2005) terms his very similar concept the *winner's attitude,* basically summarized as: "No punk is going to leave me bleeding in the street; I'm the one going home today." Conversely, whether engaged in a life-and-death hand-to-hand struggle with a suspect or being pinned down under gunfire, what has often contributed to the officer being killed, rather than surviving, is what Blum (2000) terms a *psychology of defeat;* that is, under tremendous, overwhelming stress, the officer seems to just give up, believing that "this is too much for me."

Thus, to survive a brutal, deadly encounter, an officer must be able to marshal every particle of his willpower and resolve, every ounce of physical and mental strength, to defeat the forces trying to overwhelm him. While operational training—firearms

proficiency, martial arts, concealment and cover—will help prepare the officer for the technical aspects of survival training,
mental conditioning for the will to survive prepares the officer
cognitively and emotionally for extreme survival crises. This
combination of rational-intuitive decision-making, temporary
adaptive denial of weakness, and powerful focus of will and effort is sometimes referred to as the *warrior mentality* (Norcross,
2003; Pinizzotto et al, 2004; Shale et al, 2003; Sherman, 2005).
In the world of stress management, this is as intense as it gets,
because here the stress involves literally whether or not you
make it out alive.

Blum (2000) has broken down the elements of *psychological
survival training* to a series of steps that I have adapted for my
law enforcement courses and training seminars, with a number
modifications noted here. Remember, like all the techniques
discussed in this chapter and in this book, the idea is to initially
practice under relatively low-stress conditions, then gradually
apply the skills in more and more challenging situations until
they become automatic and "second nature" even under extreme stress.

Extreme Imagery I:
The "Loved-Ones-in-Danger" Scenario

The first step involves using the attention and arousal control
strategies learned in Chapters 3 and 4 to induce a state of optimum level of arousal and attentional focus. Once you've gotten
good at these skills, under most circumstances you'll be able to
turn them on and off at will. The next skill to be called into play
is imagery (Chapter 5). In this particular application, image the
most important thing in the world to you, something that would
not only be worth fighting for, not only be worth dying for, but
worth *living for,* worth surviving and continuing to struggle
against the odds long after you think your energy is gone and
your will drained away.

For most officers, this involves images of their loved ones in
danger. Image one or more of these people in mortal peril:
threatened by criminals, attacked by terrorists, trapped in a

burning building. Use all of your well-practiced powers of sensory and cognitive imagery to conjure up the full scene of danger. This may be hard to do at first precisely because it is so unpleasant to imagine your loved ones being threatened in this manner. In fact, the more successful you are in evoking this imagery, the more distasteful it may seem, because it actually feels like *you're* the one hurting them, just by creating the scene in your mind. But stick with it. The goal is to be able to create a mental state so ferociously determined that nothing—*nothing*—short of your being cold stone dead, will deter your will to survive and protect your loved ones.

Feel it all: the raging adrenalin, the clenching muscles, the pounding heart, the lead ball in your stomach. Now image yourself saving your loved ones in danger. Mentally fight off the thugs who have them tied up; carry them in your arms from the burning vehicle; lift the fallen tree branch off them; rip through the rubble of the bombed office building to free them. Do whatever it takes in your imagination, because that's sure as hell what you'd do in real life.

Now, image yourself having successfully saved your loved ones from attack and danger: hugging them, feeling the relief and pride in having overcome impossible odds to do the right thing. Make this part of the mental imagery exercise as vivid as possible. Feel their sweaty embraces and their wet tears of joy; hear their voices rise and fall. Be the hero—you've earned it. Let the relief flush away the excess adrenalin and allow yourself to relax, aided by the arousal-regulation strategies learned in Chapter 3.

Why use this loved-ones-in-danger scenario for a mental practice module? The reason is simply that, for most people, even most police officers, real-life, extreme life-and-death situations are actually quite rare. That's the good news. The bad news from a training standpoint is that there are very few "test cases" on which to hone these psychological survival skills. So you essentially create your own simulation training scenarios, remembering, of course, always to keep it realistic. The better you can learn to mentally evoke and anticipate the overwhelming and conflicting emotions of sheer terror, boiling rage, and fierce determination, using an example of something that's categorically important to you, the better you'll be able to channel these emotions into real-life action if and when an actual law enforcement emergency arises.

Extreme Imagery II:
Police Emergency Scenarios

When you've mastered the loved-ones-in-jeopardy scenario in all its emotional vividness, the next step is to create a multi-sensory mental simulation of a work-related police scenario in which you are responding to a call of uncertain danger. Image yourself walking or driving to the scene. Use any relevant past experiences in your own career to give the image vividness and credibility. Feel the uncertainty, the combination of fear and exhilaration, as you scan the environment for signs of danger.

Now, image yourself being ambushed, jumped or cold-cocked from around a corner or behind a piece of furniture. Feel the shock and initial fear with all your senses. Image yourself being thrown to the ground, and feel the suspect trying to pin and overpower you, trying to snatch your weapon. Feel the initial helplessness as you first realize your vulnerability and reel from the unexpected blows, uncertain about what to do next. Vividly image a group of suspects holding you down, pinning you so you can't move, holding a knife at your throat, pummeling you with a brick, or choking you with an extension cord. Feel that initial sinking feeling of panic and helplessness, as you wonder if you'll ever make it out alive, ever see your loved ones again—"Holy shit, I'm gonna die."

Now explode. Go ballistic—you're dead anyway, what the fuck have you got to lose? Experience yourself filling up with inhuman rage and hatred against the scumbags who would take it all from you. Fight back with everything you've got—it's your goddamn life or theirs. Forget pain, forget fear—if they're truly threatening your life, *kill* the bastards. See the grimace on the suspect's face, smell the sweat, feel the warm drops of blood. Your attitude is: "No punk is going to leave me dying in the street. I'm the one going home today" (Garner, 2005). Visualize yourself fighting back, seizing the advantage, fear turning into confidence as the assailant is deterred, then overpowered, by you. Feel the exhilaration as you turn deadly defeat into victory.

Okay, hold it. Take a breath. I hope you understand that the purpose of this exercise is NOT to encourage the use of excessive force, nor to impel you to rash action when the best course may be to wait and bide your time, as in a hostage situation or armed standoff. Indeed, a guiding theme of law enforcement psychological training (Miller, 2006*l*) is that many confrontations can and should be prevented and defused before they turn violent— when possible. So this imagined fight-or-die scenario represents an absolute last resort tactic, an exercise designed to prepare you for that extreme, and hopefully rare, situation, where your very life is in immediate danger: you are about to be killed here and now; you have nothing to lose, so fight like hell. But even fighting like hell doesn't justify gratuitous punishment of a suspect when he has been adequately subdued and the danger is past. Remember—he's the scumbag, you're still the professional.

Also remember that fighting like hell doesn't mean forgetting your tactical combat training and just flailing around. On the contrary: here's where all those hours of real-life combat practice (ITTS) finally pay off. Fight hard but fight smart. Even in the most extreme situation, your most effective weapon is still your brain. In training, strive to simulate as many different variations of the scenario as possible: the more mentally prepared you are for different possibilities, the better. Duran (1999) believes that such mental scenarios should always end with you victorious, but don't make it *too* easy: come up with more and more complex and dangerous twists and turns that you mentally rehearse yourself overcoming. For example, image yourself making a potentially fatal mistake—Oh, shit!—but then making a deft course correction that saves your ass and allows you to triumph. Just remember to keep it realistic and to combine these mental exercises with real-life scenario training.

As you might expect, this exercise generates a great deal of emotion in my courses and training seminars. Often, the first few tries dissolve into nervous laughter, as the officers' natural defensiveness tries to deflect this unpleasant, albeit imaginary, confrontation with their own mortality. But once they get into it, it gets intense. The cops sweat, they squirm in their seats, and even an occasional chuckle can't break the concentrated spell of this exercise. It's precisely because it may be hard to put yourself completely into this extreme imaginary situation the first few times you try it, that you must keep practicing it. The whole point is to make the imaginary emergency real enough so that should you ever encounter a *really* real life-and-death emergency, you won't be overcome by the novelty and intensity of the experience—that is, you won't be cold-cocked by your own lack of training, and mental preparation.

Controlling the Scene

Finally—out of the head and onto the field. In this phase of training, we transition from mental exercises to real-life training scenarios. Remember one of the core themes of this book: The best stress management strategy is proper training, experience, and confidence. Once the mental skills of this chapter have been practiced and mastered, it is now time to apply them to the following aspects of controlling a scene (Blum, 2000). In so doing, you combine mental practice with real-life practice, so that your response to an emergency situation may include any of the following.

Seize the initiative

Initiative control refers to the process of taking control of a subject or command of a situation as soon as possible when coming into a critical scene. It is literally "seizing the initiative" by acting first. An example would be surprising and drawing down on an armed suspect and commanding him to drop his weapon before he has time to react.

React with resolve

Sometimes, however, you may be the one surprised, suddenly finding yourself in a definite OSS ("oh-shit situation"). In such circumstances, when you can't act proactively, it is vital that you bounce back as quickly and as forcefully as you can, that you do everything possible to gain *reactive control* of the situation. For example, if you're jumped by a suspect, you must be able to engage your martial arts and takedown tactics smoothly and instantaneously to regain control. Some situations may call for an explosive response, while others may require you to wait and bide your time, such as in a standoff with a barricaded armed subject (Garner, 2005; Haughton, 2005). But even the seemingly passive act of waiting can constitute a proactive response if you use the time to calculate options and strategies to employ when the opportunity presents itself.

Adapt expertly

How smoothly you are able to bring your skills into play is determined by your level of *adaptive expertise,* which is the product of ongoing training and practice in as many diverse situations as possible. This involves both direct skill training and the kind of mental preparation training described in this chapter. Contributors to adaptive expertise include *accurate expectations* about what to expect in most kinds of critical incident settings, *awareness and presence of mind* achieved by utilizing many of the attention and arousal control strategies discussed earlier, and *confidence* in your ability to handle virtually anything they can throw at you because you have trained, practiced, and are mentally and physically prepared for action. The subject of expertise has been discussed more fully in Chapter 2.

Officer Survival Training

Now, it's time to put it all together, to describe an overall protocol for managing extreme stress in critical situations and emerging victorious. This *Officer Survival Training* protocol (Blum, 2000) includes the following integrated components:

> *Stay in condition.* This involves keeping your body and mind in peak condition, maintaining your physical and psychological health and fitness.

Train. Acquire and maintain familiarity and proficiency with tactics, procedures, and equipment relevant to your law enforcement work = ITTS.

Plan. Develop and rehearse tactical plans that can be adapted to as many types of diverse scenarios as possible. Only in this way can officers build the confidence that will enable them to think decisively and act effectively in emergency crisis situations.

Do it. Here, you actually practice the tactics and strategies under as many kinds of real and simulated conditions as possible.

Communicate and coordinate. Most successful police operations, such as hostage negotiation, undercover operations, or SWAT (Miller, 2005e, 2006j, 2006*l*), require tight coordination among many team members, so it is important to establish clear lines and methods of communication and teamwork under what might be very difficult conditions.

Cop (no pun intended) the right attitude. As this chapter has hopefully made clear, "attitude" is not some ephemeral, airy-fairy, psychobabble, throwaway concept, but an indispensable ingredient in the will to survive and prevail in a deadly encounter. To reiterate: a proper, confident, assertive attitude is fostered by utilizing the mental toughness training exercises in these chapters, but it depends vitally on practical nuts-and-bolts skills training to provide a realistic basis for that confidence— ITTS rules!

PART III:

Post-Incident Mental Toughness Reinforcement

8

Critical Incidents Stress and the Stress Response

In the preceding chapters, we've talked about Mental Toughness Training in terms of preparation, or what we called primary and secondary prevention in Chapter 1; that is, what you can do ahead of time to inoculate yourself against overwhelming stress and trauma on the job, and how to prepare for and deal with a potentially overwhelming and life-threatening confrontation.

But even with the best training, practice, and mental preparation, we're still human, and it would be unrealistic to expect no adverse reaction after a critical incident. Just as strengthening the body against impact doesn't guarantee you'll be totally impervious to injury, mentally toughening yourself won't guarantee that you'll experience no stress response at all. And just like it's not too late to intervene and hasten recovery from a physical injury after it occurs, the METTLE program applies as well to follow-up measures that officers can utilize to assure that stress reactions don't spin out of control and to afford the quickest and most complete recovery possible; this is the concept of tertiary prevention discussed in Chapter 1.

The present chapter discusses the concept of critical incident stress and the various reactions to it that officers may have, and the next two chapters describe group and individual interventions that have proven valuable in maintaining and reinforcing an officer's mental toughness following a critical incident. Subsequent chapters will deal with specific law enforcement challenges and critical incidents in more detail.

99

Critical Incidents and the
Posttraumatic Stress Response

Critical Incident Stress

A *critical incident* is defined as any event that has an unusually powerful, negative impact on personnel. In the present context, it is any event that a law enforcement officer may experience that exceeds the range of the ordinary stresses and hassles that come with the job. Of course, the definition of "ordinary" depends on what type of law enforcement assignment you have. Ordinary stresses for a traffic patrol or community policing officer may be different from ordinary stresses for a SWAT team member or hostage negotiator. But when an incident occurs that is above and beyond a particular officer's usual experience, it may qualify as a critical incident.

For most officers, major classes of critical incidents include: a line-of-duty death; serious injury to police personnel; a serious multiple-casualty incident such as a multiple school shooting or workplace violence incident; the suicide of a fellow police officer; the traumatic death of children, especially where irresponsible or frankly malevolent adults were involved; an event with excessive media interest; or a victim who is a family member or otherwise well-known to one or more responding officers (Mitchell & Everly, 1996, 2003). Recent times have multiplied exponentially the range and scope of horrific law enforcement critical incidents to include acts of mass terror and destruction, involving multiple deaths of civilians, fellow officers, and other emergency personnel (Henry, 2004; Karlsson & Christianson, 2003; Miller, 1998d, 1999b; 2000a, 2000b, 2002b, 2004b, 2005a, 2006c, 2006d, in press-b, in press-d; Regher & Bober, 2004).

Susceptibility to stressful events varies among different persons, and most individuals are able to resolve acute critical incident stress through the use of informal social support and other adaptive activities (Bowman, 1997; Carlier & Gersons, 1995; Carlier et al, 1997; Gentz, 1991). However, critical incident stress that is not resolved adequately or treated appropriately in the first few days or weeks may develop into one or more forms of psychological *traumatic disability syndrome* (Miller, 1998d). The best known of these is *posttraumatic stress disorder*, or PTSD.

Posttraumatic Stress Disorder (PTSD)

The concept of critical incident stress grew out of the larger tradition of trauma psychology. Although persisting and debilitating stress reactions to wartime and civilian traumas have been recorded for centuries (Trimble, 1981; Wilson, 1994), *posttraumatic stress disorder* (PTSD) first achieved status as a codified psychiatric syndrome as recently as 1980 (APA, 1980), and is still today only reluctantly coming to be accepted as a legitimate medical casualty in wartime and civilian combat (Clary, 2005; Corbett, 2004; Galovski & Lyons, 2004; Nordland & Gegax, 2004; Paton & Smith, 1999; Tyre, 2004; see also Chapter 1). A number of other types of psychological syndromes, which don't meet the full clinical criteria of PTSD, may also follow exposure to traumatic events; these include phobias, anxiety, panic attacks, depression, and substance abuse problems (Miller, 1994b, 1998b).

Diagnostically, PTSD is described as a syndrome of cognitive, emotional, and behavioral disturbance following exposure to a traumatic stressor that injures or threatens oneself or others, and that involves the experience of intense fear, helplessness, or horror (APA, 2000; Meek, 1990; Merskey, 1992; Modlin, 1983, 1990; Weiner, 1992). As a result, following a law enforcement critical incident, there may develop a characteristic set of PTSD symptoms, which can include any of the following.

Anxiety. The officer experiences a continual state of free-floating anxiety and maintains an intense hypervigilance, scanning the environment for impending threats of danger. Panic attacks may be occasional or frequent.

Physiological arousal. The officer's nervous system is on continual alert, producing increased bodily tension in the form of muscle tightness, tremors, restlessness, heightened startle response, fatigue, heart palpitations, breathing difficulties, dizziness, headaches, or other physical symptoms.

Irritability. There is a pervasive edginess, impatience, loss of humor, and quick anger over seemingly trivial matters. Friends and coworkers may get annoyed and shun the officer, while family members may feel abused and alienated. Interactions with citizens on patrol may grow testy and lead to unwarranted confrontations.

Avoidance/denial. The officer tries to blot out the event from his mind. He avoids thinking or talking about the traumatic event, as well as news items, conversations, TV shows, or even interaction with coworkers that remind him of the incident. Part of this is a deliberate, conscious effort to avoid trauma-reminders, while part involves an involuntary psychic numbing that blunts incoming threatening stimuli. On the job, the officer may "lie low," minimizing his contact with the public and his fellow officers, and thereby underperform in his law enforcement duties.

Intrusion. Despite the officer's best efforts to keep the traumatic event out of his mind, the disturbing incident pushes its way into consciousness, typically in the form of intrusive images or flashbacks by day and/or frightening dreams at night.

Repetitive nightmares. Sometimes the officer's nightmares replay the actual traumatic event; more commonly, the dreams echo the general theme and emotional intensity of the trauma, but partially disguise the actual event in terms of content. For example, one officer who was jumped and beaten by a suspect in an unlighted room reported recurring dreams of "tripping over a rock and being bit by a snake."

Impaired concentration and memory. Friends and family may notice that the officer has become a "space cadet," while supervisors report deteriorating work performance because the officer "can't concentrate on doing his job."

Social and recreational functioning may be impaired as the officer has difficulty remembering names, loses the train of conversations, or can't keep his mind focused on reading material or games.

Withdrawal/isolation. The officer shuns friends, school-mates, and family members, having no tolerance for the petty, trivial concerns of everyday life. The hurt feelings this engenders in others may spur resentment and counter avoidance, leading to a vicious cycle of mutual rejection and eventual social ostracism of the officer.

Acting-out. More rarely, the traumatized officer may walk off his patrol, wander out of his familiar jurisdiction, or take unaccustomed risks by driving too fast, hanging out with unsavory characters on his beat (or within his own department), gambling, using substances, being insubordinate, or acting recklessly with suspects and citizens, thereby putting himself or other officers in unnecessary danger.

Delayed, Displaced, or Prolonged Reactions

In some cases, especially if no treatment or other appropriate support has been provided, the aftereffects of a traumatic inci-dent may persist for many months or longer in the form of anger, hostility, irritability, fatigue, inability to concentrate, loss of self-confidence, neglect of health, increased indulgence in food or substances, or problems with authority and discipline. Many of these long-term effects obviously will interfere with work performance and threaten the stability of close personal relationships. Ultimately, they may be responsible for early re-tirement, burnout, or even suicide (Bohl, 1991, 1995; Cum-mings, 1996; Miller, 2005d, 2006a).

In some cases, an officer may appear to emerge from a danger-ous situation or series of emergencies emotionally unscathed, only to later break down and develop a full-blown PTSD reac-tion following a relatively minor incident like a traffic accident (Davis & Breslau, 1994). The fender-bender, certainly far less traumatic than the grim scenes encountered in emergency work, seems to have vividly symbolized the personal risk, sense of human fragility, and existential uncertainty that the officer's professional activities entail but that he is unable to face directly if he is to maintain his necessary adaptive defenses and get his job done. This stuffed, built-up emotion may then be projected onto the minor incident because it is a "safer" target to break down or blow up at. Unfortunately, this may cause him to fear that he's losing control or going crazy, which further increases his fear but unfortunately makes him even more reluctant to report it. Here, alert family members, coworkers, or supervisors may have to step in to urge the stricken officer to get the help he or she needs.

Risk and Resiliency Factors for PTSD

As noted previously, not everyone who experiences a traumatic critical incident has the same reaction or develops the same degree of psychological disability, and there is significant variability among individual levels of susceptibility and resilience to stressful events (Bowman, 1997; Paton et al, 2003).

Risk factors for PTSD or other traumatic disability syndromes in officers may be:

Biological, including genetic predisposition and inborn heightened physiological reactivity to stimuli.

Historical, such as prior exposure to trauma or other co-existing adverse life circumstances.

Psychological, including poor coping and problem-solving skills, learned helplessness, and a history of dysfunctional interpersonal relationships.

Environmental/contextual, such as inadequate departmental or societal support (Carlier, 1999; Paton & Smith, 1999; Paton et al, 2000; Regehr & Bober, 2004).

Equally important, but too often overlooked, are resiliency factors that enable officers to withstand and even prevail in the face of seemingly overwhelming trauma (Paton et al, 2000).

Recent research (Bonanno, 2005, Tedeschi & Kilmer, 2005) has identified three major dimensions of resiliency:

> *Recovery* is characterized by moderate to severe initial psychological symptoms that significantly disrupt normal functioning and that decline gradually before returning to pre-trauma levels.

> *Resilience* is characterized by relatively mild and short-lived disruptions in normal functioning, with a relatively quick recovery to baseline.

> *Posttraumatic growth* describes a state in which survivors report being significantly changed or transformed by their struggle with adversity. Somehow, by coping with this major life event, they discover strengths and qualities within themselves and in the world around them that actually seem to make their lives richer and more meaningful. This doesn't mean that they leave all of their distress behind. Indeed, many survivors indicate that they are still suffering from the aftermath of the trauma; however, a common theme is an increased sense of their own capacities to survive and prevail (Tedeschi & Kilmer, 2005).

Resiliency factors specific to law enforcement include superior training and skill development; a learning attitude toward the profession; good verbal and interpersonal skills; higher intelligence; adequate emotional control; optimism; good problem-solving and adaptive coping skills; and the ability and willingness to seek help and support where necessary (Miller, 1998d, 2006l; Paton et al, 2000). Proper intervention services for PTSD and other critical incident stress reactions should make good use of these inherent resiliency factors wherever possible as part of the overall program of Mental Toughness Training. It is to these post-incident, resiliency-enhancing measures that we now turn.

9

Tough Group Debriefing Models

"You're not crazy"

In providing secondary and tertiary prevention strategies to law enforcement and emergency services personnel who have experienced stressful critical incidents, a key element involves de-pathologizing and de-stigmatizing their reactions and promoting, where possible, the support and encouragement of their colleagues: "Others have walked in your shoes and survived." In addition to officers themselves, this chapter and the next should be read by clinicians and counselors who work with law enforcement personnel, as they describe the types of effective mental health interventions that are consistent with the resiliency-building METTLE model.

Critical Incident Stress Debriefing: Models and Methods

Critical incident stress debriefing (CISD) is a structured group intervention designed to promote the emotional processing of traumatic events through the ventilation and normalization of reactions, as well as to facilitate preparation for possible future crisis experiences. Although initially designed for use in groups, variations of the CISD approach have also been used with individuals, couples, and families. CISD is actually one component of an integrated, comprehensive crisis intervention program spanning the critical incident continuum from pre-crisis, to crisis, to post-crisis phases, and subsumed under the heading of *critical incident stress management (CISM),* which has been adopted and modified for law enforcement and emergency services departments throughout the United States, Great Britain, Europe, Australia, and other parts of the world (Dyregrov, 1989, 1997; Everly & Mitchell, 1997; Everly et al, 2000; Miller, 1995, 1998d, 1999b, 1999d, 2006c, in press-a, in press-c; Mitchell & Everly, 1996, 2003).

The full CISM program includes: individual and organizational *pre-crisis preparation*; large-scale *demobilization* procedures following mass disasters; on-scene, *one-on-one supportive counseling* for acute, individual crisis reactions; *defusings*, which represent a shorter, compressed stress debriefing protocol for small groups under acute stress; *critical incident stress debriefing*, described more extensively below; *family crisis intervention* and supportive counseling; and referral for *follow-up mental health services* as needed (Everly & Mitchell, 1997; Mitchell & Everly, 1996, 2003).

Indications for CISD

There are a number of criteria by which peer support or command staff might decide to provide a CISD to law enforcement personnel following a critical incident: many officers within a department or interagency work team appear to be distressed after a particular call; the signs of stress appear to be quite severe; officers demonstrate significant behavioral changes and/or disruption of work performance; officers directly request help (less common, in my experience); or the event is unusual or extraordinary in some other respect (Mitchell & Bray, 1990; Mitchell & Everly, 1996, 2003).

Structure of the Debriefings

A CISD debriefing is a peer-led, clinician-guided process, although the individual roles of clinicians and peers may vary from setting to setting. The staffing of a debriefing usually consists of a mental health clinician and one or more peer debriefers, i.e. fellow police officers, firefighters, paramedics, or other crisis workers who have been trained in the CISD process and who may have been through critical incidents and debriefings in their own careers.

A typical debriefing takes place within 24 to 72 hours of the critical incident and consists of a single group meeting that lasts two to three hours, although shorter or longer meetings may be dictated by circumstances. Group size may range from a handful to a roomful, the determining factor usually being how many people will have time to fully express themselves in the number of hours allotted for the debriefing. Typical group debriefings last approximately 2–3 hours. Where large numbers of personnel are involved, such as in mass disaster rescues, several debriefings may be held successively over the course of days to accommodate all of the personnel involved (Everly & Mitchell, 1997; Mitchell & Everly, 1996, 2003).

The formal CISD process—often referred to as the *Mitchell model* or the *ICISF model,* after its originator, Jeffrey Mitchell of the International Critical Incident Stress Foundation—consists of seven key phases, designed to assist psychological integration, beginning with more objective and descriptive levels of processing, progressing to the more personal and emotional, and back to the educative and integrative levels, focusing on both cognitive and emotional mastery of the traumatic event.

Introduction. The introduction phase of a debriefing is the time when the team leader—either a mental health professional or peer debriefer, depending on the composition of the group—gradually introduces the CISD process, encourages participation by the group, and sets the ground rules by which the debriefing will operate. These guidelines include confidentiality, attendance for the full session, unforced participation in the discussions, and the establishment of a noncritical atmosphere.

Fact phase. During this phase, the group members are asked to briefly describe their job or role during the critical incident and, from their own perspective, provide some facts about what happened. The basic question is: "What did you do?"

Thought phase. The CISD leader asks the group members to discuss their initial and subsequent thoughts during the critical incident: "What was going through your mind?"

Reaction phase. This phase is designed to move the group participants from a predominantly cognitive mode of processing to a more expressive emotional level: "What was the worst part of the incident for you?" It is usually at this point that the meeting gets intense, as members take their cue from one another and begin to vent their distress. Clinicians and peer-debriefers keep a keen eye out for any adverse or unusual reactions among the personnel.

Symptom phase. This begins the movement back from the predominantly emotional processing level toward the cognitive processing level. Participants are asked to describe cognitive, physical, emotional, and behavioral signs of distress that appeared immediately at the scene or within several hours of the incident, a few days after the incident, and may still persist at the time of the debriefing: "What have you been experiencing since the incident?"

Education phase. Continuing the move back toward intellectual processing, didactic information is provided about the nature of the stress response and the expected physiological and psychological reactions to critical incidents. This serves to normalize the stress and coping responses and to provide a basis for questions and answers.

Re-entry phase. This is the wrap-up, during which any additional questions or statements are addressed, referral for individual follow-ups are made, and general group bonding is reinforced: "What have you learned?" "Is there anything positive that can come out of this experience that can help you grow personally or professionally?" "How can you help one another in the future?" "Anything we left out?"

This is not to suggest that these phases always follow one another in an unvarying, mechanical sequence. In my experience, once group participants feel comfortable with the debriefing process and start talking, there is often a tendency for the fact, thought, and reaction phases to blend together. Indeed, as Mitchell & Everly (1996, 2003) recognize, it would seem artificial and forced to abruptly interrupt someone expressing emotion just because "it's not the right phase." As long as the basic rationale and structure of the debriefing are maintained, the beneficial effect will usually result. Indeed, on a number of occasions, previously silent members have spoken up at literally the last moment, when the group was all but getting up to leave. Clinician team leaders typically have to intervene only when emotional reactions become particularly intense, or where one or more members begin to blame or criticize others.

For a successful debriefing, timing and clinical appropriateness are important. The consensus from the literature and my own clinical experience support the scheduling of debriefings toward the earlier end of the recommended 24–72 hour window (Bordow & Porritt, 1979; Miller, 1995, 1998d, 1999b, 2006c; Solomon & Benbenishty, 1988). To keep the focus on the event itself and to reduce the potential for singling-out individuals, some authorities recommend that there be a policy of mandatory referral of all involved personnel to a debriefing or other appropriate mental health intervention (Horn, 1991; McMains, 1991; Mitchell, 1991; Reese, 1991; Solomon, 1988, 1990, 1995). However, in other cases, mandatory or enforced CISD may lead to passive participation and resentment among the conscripted personnel (Bisson & Deahl, 1994; Flannery et al, 1991), and the CISD process may quickly become a stale routine if used indiscriminately after every incident, thereby diluting its effectiveness in those situations where it really could have helped. Departmental supervisors and mental health consultants must use their common sense and knowledge of their own personnel to make these kinds of judgment calls.

Special Applications of CISD for Law Enforcement

Police officers tend to be an insular group and reluctant to talk to outsiders. At the same time, they may be more resistant to showing vulnerability and weakness in front of their own peers than are other emergency personnel. Cops typically work alone or with a single partner, unlike firefighters and paramedics who are trained to have more of a team mentality (Blau, 1994; Miller, 1995, 1999d, 2006c, in press-c; Reese, 1987; Solomon, 1995). This has led to some special adaptations of the CISD approach for law enforcement.

Law Enforcement Debriefing

Perhaps the most extensive and comprehensive adaptation of the CISD process for law enforcement comes from the work of police psychologist Nancy Bohl (1995) who explicitly compares and contrasts the phases in her own program with the phases of the ICISF model of CISD.

In Bohl's program, the debriefing takes place as soon after the critical incident as possible. A debriefing may involve a single officer within the first 24 hours, later followed by a second individual debriefing, with a follow-up group debriefing taking place within one week to encourage group cohesion and bonding. This addresses the occupationally lower team orientation of most police officers who may not express feelings easily, even— or especially—in a group of their fellow cops.

The Bohl model makes no real distinction between the cognitive and emotional phases of a debriefing. If an officer begins to express emotion during the fact or cognitive phase, there is little point in telling him or her to stifle it until later. To be fair, the ICISF model certainly does allow for flexibility and common sense in structuring debriefings, and both formats recognize the importance of responding empathically to the specific needs expressed by the participants, rather than just following a rigid set of rules.

In the emotion phase itself, what is important in the Bohl model is not the mere act of venting, but rather the opportunity to validate feelings. Bohl does not ask what the "worst thing" was, since she finds that the typical officer's response is likely to be that "everything about it was the worst thing." However, it often comes as a revelation to these law enforcement tough guys that their peers have had similar feelings.

Still, some emotions may be difficult to validate. For example, guilt or remorse over acts of commission or omission during the incident may have some basis in reality, as when an officer's momentary hesitation or impulsive action resulted in someone getting hurt or killed. In Bohl's model, the question then becomes: "Okay, you feel guilty—what are you going to do with that guilt?" That is, "What can be learned from the experience to prevent something like this from happening again?" This, of course, is the essence of the 20/20/20 principle from Chapter 1.

The Bohl debriefing model includes an additional phase, termed *unfinished business*, which has no formal counterpart in the ICISF model. Participants are asked, "What in the present situation reminds you of past experiences? Do you want to talk about those other situations?" This phase grew out of Bohl's observation that the incident prompting the current debriefing often acts as a catalyst for recalling past traumatic events. The questions give participants a chance to talk about these prior incidents that may arouse strong, unresolved feelings. Bohl finds that such multilevel debriefings result in a greater sense of relief and closure than might occur by sticking solely to the present incident. This jives with my own experience that, during an ongoing debriefing, feelings and reactions to past critical incidents will sometimes spontaneously come up and this must be dealt with and worked through as it arises (Miller, 1995, 1999b, 2000a, 2000b, 2006c, in press-c). However, team leaders must be careful not to lose too much of the structure and focus of the current debriefing.

The education phase in the Bohl model resembles its ICISF model counterpart, in that participants are schooled about normal and pathological stress reactions, how to deal with coworkers and family members, and what to anticipate in the days and weeks ahead. For example, an officer's child may have heard that his or her parent shot and killed a suspect, and the child may be questioned or teased at school (Kirschman, 1997; Miller, 1998d, 2006k, 2006*l*, 2007). How to deal with children's responses may therefore be an important part of this education phase.

Unlike the ICISF model, the Bohl model does not ask whether anything positive, hopeful, or growth-promoting has arisen from the incident. Officers who have seen their partners shot or killed or who have had to deal with child abuse or other senseless brutality ought to be given some slack for failing to perceive anything "positive" about the incident. In these circumstances, expecting them to extract some kind of existential growth experience from such an event may seem like a sick joke. On the other hand, as discussed in Chapter 8, this kind of posttraumatic growth sometimes does occur—spontaneously or with gentle guidance—in the wake of a horrible event (Almedom, 2005; Dunning, 1999; Stuhlmiller & Dunning, 2000; Tedeschi & Calhoun, 1995; Tedeschi & Kilmer, 2005; Violanti, 2000). In such cases, it should be nurtured and encouraged, but should never be presented as an expectation that might set the officer up for further disappointment and self-reproach (Miller, 1998d, 2006*l*).

A final non-ICISF phase of the Bohl debriefing model is the *round robin* in which each officer is invited to say essentially whatever he or she feels like. The statement can be addressed to anyone or to no one in particular, but others cannot respond directly, which is supposed to give participants a feeling of safety. My own concern is that this may provide an opportunity for last-minute gratuitous sniping, which can quickly erode the supportive atmosphere that has been carefully crafted during the debriefing. Additionally, in practice, there doesn't seem to be anything particularly unique about this round robin phase to distinguish it from the standard re-entry phase of the Mitchell model. Finally, adding more and more "phases" to the debriefing process may serve to decrease the forthrightness and spontaneity of its implementation. As always, clinical judgment and common sense should guide the process.

Integrative Debriefing

Bohl (1995) has sought to preserve the essential structure and philosophy of the ICISF debriefing model, while fine-tuning the technique for specific application to law enforcement populations. Similarly, Regehr and colleagues (Regehr, 2001; Regehr & Bober 2004) have proposed a debriefing protocol that purportedly builds on the strengths of earlier models, while modifying elements that may be counter-productive. They note that a closely related approach was used in working with survivors of the September 11th, 2001, Pentagon terrorists' attack (Ruzek, 2002). This model contains the following phases:

Introduction. The group begins with a discussion of the purpose of the meeting and an expression of support for the members who have shared a traumatic experience. The group leaders are introduced and ground rules for respectful interaction are outlined.

Shared understanding. It is not uncommon for debriefing team leaders and/or participants to have incomplete or confusing understanding of the critical incident in questions and the circumstances surrounding it. To provide a common ground for the session, several authorities (Dyregrov, 1997; Everly et al, 2000; Mitchell & Everly, 1993, 1996; Regehr, 2001) recommend a kind of "pre-debriefing briefing" to bone up on the facts of the case. As a guilty party on a few occasions, I can attest to the embarrassment and erosion of credibility that can result from lack of preparation of this nature. Not everything can be known, of course, but a common understanding of the event in question puts everyone on the same page to facilitate communication. As a rule, law enforcement and emergency services personnel experience lower levels of physiological arousal and distress when provided with properly timed and accurate information.

Impact of experience. The effects of the critical incident are discussed, including current emotional, physical, and cognitive symptoms experienced by participants.

Special attention is also paid to the impact on relationships with family and friends, a topic often glossed over in many traditional debriefings. Similar to the symptom and teaching phases of a standard ICISF debriefing, team leaders normalize the reactions through education and by identifying commonalities among the experiences of group members. Families and friends continue to be the most important resource for these personnel, and efforts must be made to ensure that they do not become alienated in the aftermath of a traumatic event (Miller, 1998d, 2006*l*).

Strategies for coping. Group members are invited to share their strategies for coping, describe what has worked and what has not, and to make suggestions to one another regarding effective symptom management. Team leaders validate the ingenuity and resourcefulness of the self-help and mutual aid efforts of the participants and then refine and extend these techniques by presenting further cognitive-behavioral strategies for managing symptoms and adverse reactions. Teaching officers specific skills to deal with distressing symptoms helps them attain a sense of mastery and feel less out of control.

Mobilizing social supports. Team leaders capitalize on the group cohesion and solidarity of the debriefing to encourage the participants to continue supporting one another and to further solidify and expand the existing network of social supports. Regehr & Bober (2004) wisely caution that this kind of support-building must be developed in the context of an existing positive working relationship with the organization and its members. Few things more gallingly provoke cynicism and demoralization than trying to force-feed a bogus sense of camaraderie to a group characterized by a past record of conflict and bad blood. In general, the creation of an organizational climate that supports personnel and induces a sense of trust serves as a general moderator of stress reactions during and following a traumatic event (Miller, 1994b, 1995, 1998d).

Wrap-up. The participants are thanked for their willingness to engage and share. Strengths are reinforced and opportunities for follow-up are provided. Where indicated, the most distressed officers must be encouraged and supported to utilize additional mental heath care.

Line-of-Duty Death Debriefing

Mitchell & Levenson (2006) have recently elaborated a specialized law enforcement debriefing model for officers coping with a *line-of-duty death* (LODD)—perhaps the ultimate stressor for both individual officers and the department as a whole (Henry, 2004; Miller, in press-a). They point out that on the day of the LODD, a full seven-phase CISD is probably far too emotionally overwhelming for most personnel who have just endured the death of a colleague and friend. In this view, the full seven-phase ICISF-model CISD process should be postponed for three to seven days following the slain officer's funeral.

Meanwhile, the immediate post-LODD debriefing is modified into a streamlined, five-phase protocol that is conducted on the day of the death and usually lasts between 30 and 45 minutes. Its objectives are to disseminate accurate information about the incident and its aftermath and to prepare the personnel to face the turmoil of the next few days, as they go through the funeral and mourning process. Additionally, it is helpful in guiding people in self-care and "buddy support" as they deal with the loss of a colleague. The phases of the modified LODD debriefing are:

Introduction. This is kept as brief as possible. In general, for intradepartmental debriefings, everybody pretty much knows everybody already.

Fact phase. Missing or ambiguous information—"not knowing"—is almost always more stressful than the grim facts, no matter how unpleasant those may be. Officers who were present during the LODD are asked to briefly describe what happened so that others can obtain at least the most basic and pertinent facts about the situation.

Reaction phase. The participants are asked, "What are you having the most difficulty with right now?" The rationale is that the overall "worst part" of the situation (as is asked in the traditional debriefing model) typically cannot yet be solicited because, at this early point, most of the officers are still emotionally raw and/or numb and haven't had time to come to grips with what the overall worst part may turn out to be. For many, the worst part will occur during or after the funeral.

Teaching phase. The teaching phase is used to prepare officers for the funeral and to encourage them to do things that will help them to take care of themselves as they cope with this loss.

Reentry phase. For the most part, this is a question, answer, and summarization process to help officers move forward and cope with the effects of the tragedy in the weeks and months ahead.

In Mitchell & Levenson's (2006) two-part model, the full seven-phase CISD is usually provided three to seven days later as a follow-up to the streamlined five-phase CISD that was provided on the day of the death.

Individual Debriefings

Mitchell & Levenson (2006) point out that LODD situations require more one-on-one interventions than almost any other situation. More broadly, in cases where only one officer is involved in any kind of critical incident, or as an individual precursor or follow-up to a formal group debriefing, Solomon (1991, 1995) has recommended that individual debriefings be conducted by a trained mental health professional. In this one-on-one encounter, the emotional impact of the incident is assessed and explored as thoughts, feelings, and reactions are discussed. An effective format for individual debriefing sessions is to go over the incident "frame by frame," allowing the officer to verbalize the moment-by-moment thoughts, perceptions, sensory details, feelings, and actions that occurred during the critical incident. This format helps the officer become aware of, sort out, and make sense of what happened.

Getting in touch with the perceptions and state of mind experienced during the critical incident may help the officer understand why certain actions were taken or specific decisions were made. The frame-by-frame approach helps defuse inappropriate self-blaming by encouraging the officer to differentiate what was under his control from what was not, and what was known at the time of the incident from what was impossible to know then, but may appear crystal clear in hindsight; again, recalling the 20/20/20 principle.

Finally, as a follow-up measure, Solomon (1995) recommends a *critical incident peer support seminar,* which provides a retreat-like setting for the involved officers to come together for two or three days to revisit their experience several months following the critical incident. The seminar is facilitated by mental health professionals and peer-support officers. While this may not always be practical, it emphasizes the important role of communal support in recovering resilience after a critical incident (Miller, 1995, 1998d, 2006*l*).

Salutogenic Debriefing

One group of practitioners (Dunning, 1999; Paton et al, 2003; Stuhlmiller & Dunning, 2000; Violanti, 2000) has advocated a radical shift in the theory and practice of critical incident debriefing. Their main criticism of the standard CISD model is that it pathologizes stress reactions and offers debriefing as a quick-fix, one-size-fits-all package of therapeutic intervention. These authors propose an alternative *salutogenic debriefing* model that views critical incident reactions as opportunities for adaptive coping and personal growth.

Consistent with our discussion in Chapters 1 and 8 on recovery, resilience, and posttraumatic growth, these authors propose that interventions for critical incidents should not foster the learned helplessness of a traumatized victim mentality but should encourage a sense of competence, confidence, resilience, hardiness, and learned resourcefulness (Almedom, 2005; Antonovsky, 1987; Higgins, 1994; Kobassa et al, 1982; Miller, 1998a; Tedeschi & Calhoun, 1995; Tedeschi & Kilmer, 2005).

In fairness, the purpose of all traumatic stress interventions, including CISD, is to reduce hopelessness and helplessness and to foster adaptive and resilient coping; indeed, this emphasis is at the core of the METTLE program. But going too far in the other direction and adopting a "Clarence the Angel" approach to intervention (Miller, 1998d) may only put too much pressure on distressed officers who understandably may not be able to bring themselves to turn a horrific episode into a personal growth experience, and may therefore feel like they're being made to seem like failures if they can't meet this excessively high bar of recovery and growth. As always, clinicians and law enforcement administrators alike have to use their professional judgment.

More broadly, most authorities would endorse the idea that CISD, or any other systemized approach to intervention, should supplement and enhance—not replace—each individual's natural coping resources (McNally et al, 2003; Sheehan et al, 2004). In other words, *all* psychological services for law enforcement should be in the direction of empowering officers to deal with challenges as independently and effectively as possible (Miller, 2006*l*). While many critical incidents will not require any special intervention, and while the majority of those that do will be well served by a CISD approach, it is the responsibility of departmental administrators, and the mental health professionals who advise them, to ensure that debriefing modalities are used responsibly and that other forms of clinically appropriate psychotherapeutic intervention are available to those who need them. CISD, like all successful treatment modalities, must be a living, evolving organism. Continued research and clinical ingenuity will hopefully further texturize and expand the stress debriefing approach into new and different applications (Miller, 1999b, 2006c).

10

Tough Individual Counseling Models

As noted in Chapter 8, even with the best training, practice, and preparation, adverse reactions to law enforcement critical incidents may occur and persist. For some officers, CISD-type debriefings and other group interventions (Chapter 9) may not suffice or there may be too few officers affected by the incident for a group program to function. In such cases, more individualized approaches can be effective in reinforcing the METTLE mindset of resilient coping with stress. Accordingly, this chapter, like the last one, should be read both by law enforcement officers and the mental health clinicians who treat and advise them.

Law Enforcement Psychotherapy: The METTLE Model

Unfortunately, sometimes for good reason (Max, 2000), police officers have traditionally shunned mental health services, often perceiving its practitioners as ferrets and shills who are out to dig up dirt that their departments can use against them. Other cops may fear having their "head shrunk," harboring a notion of the psychotherapy process as akin to brainwashing, a humiliating and emasculating experience in which they are forced to lie on a couch and sob about their inner child. Less dramatically and more commonly, the idea of needing any kind of "mental help" implies weakness, cowardice, and lack of ability to do the job. In the environment of many departments, some officers realistically fear censure, stigmatization, ridicule, thwarted career advancement, and alienation from colleagues if they are perceived as the type who "folds under pressure." Still others in the department who may have something to hide may fear a colleague "spilling his guts" to the clinician and thereby blowing the malfeasor's cover (Miller, 1995, 1998d, 1999d, 2000a, 2000b, 2006*l*, in press-c).

But in the METTLE model, the goal of law enforcement psychological services following a critical incident is to help make officers *stronger*, not weaker. Sometimes a broken bone that has begun to heal crookedly has to be re-broken and reset properly for the individual to be able to walk normally again and, while the re-breaking may hurt, the pain is almost always temporary and the effect is to restore and re-strengthen the limb. In the same way, an officer who is responding to critical incident stress with a rigidly malformed defensive mindset that's screwing up his job performance and personal life, may need to have those defenses challenged in a supportive atmosphere, so he or she can benefit from a healthy "resetting" of his mental state to deal with life more adaptively and courageously. He or she needs to regain the psychological strength to learn to walk the path of life again.

And just as the officer with the reset leg fracture must undergo a course of physical therapy to rehabilitate his ambulatory function, the officer with the readjusted mental attitude may need a brief course of psych rehab to reinforce and consolidate the mental skill-set he or she will use to return to healthy functioning, and to strengthen his or her mental state for future challenges. This is what the Mental Toughness Training approach is all about.

But for this kind of psychological services model to work, it must have the support and encouragement of the police agency's administration (Miller, 1998d, 2006*l*). The clinician, the officer, and the department should all be clear at the outset about issues relating to confidentiality, privilege, duty-to-protect, and chain of command, and any changes in these ground rules should be clarified as needed. Mishandling of a psychological referral can have severe consequences for the officer and the department (Max, 2000; Miller, 2006*l*; Toch, 2002), so police administrators should make it their responsibility to assess and monitor the quality of the mental health services provided by their psychologists (Miller, 2006*l*).

Phases of Law Enforcement Psychotherapy

For officers rebounding from a specific traumatic critical incident, police psychologist Ellen Kirschman (1997) has conceptualized the therapeutic process as proceeding across two phases, which at times may overlap.

The *stabilization phase* allows the officer to gradually ratchet down the emotional intensity of the traumatic experience in order to create a secure and safe psychological environment for dealing with the effects of the critical incident. Therapeutic strategies and activities at this phase include encouraging the officer to attend a critical incident debriefing with his peers (assuming one is available) and to obtain as much information and feedback about the event as he is able to assimilate. Time off from work or assignment to light duty might ease the transition back to the officer's prior full-status work assignment. Inasmuch as many officers may be reluctant to ask for such duty for fear of seeming weak, some departments institute a mandatory waiting period until the officer is cleared by the departmental psychologist. Where appropriate, medication for mood stabilization or sleep may be helpful. Also, the officer should be encouraged to obtain as much positive psychological support as possible from friends and family, while steering clear of people who bring him down.

In the *working through* stage of therapy, the officer begins to find meaning in what happened to him and to integrate the experience into his belief system and worldview. In constructing such a personal narrative, some elements of the experience and his reactions to it may fit into his existing worldview; in other cases, his core beliefs may have to be expanded or amended to accommodate the traumatic event. Officers may have to mourn the parts of themselves that have been lost as a result of the traumatic experience and develop plans for the future that stake out new territory in terms of their roles as officers, family members, citizens, and so on.

In practice, psychotherapy typically proceeds in the form of a cyclical flywheel, with alternating starts and stops, forward thrusts and backslides, so clinicians need not get too hung up on doing things in the "right order"—recall the similar point made about the debriefing phases in Chapter 9. But as with debriefings, flexibility in individual counseling doesn't mean that "anything goes" and, to be effective, law enforcement psychotherapy should always retain some guiding structure and should incorporate a number of essential components (Miller, 1998d, 2006*l*), which are described below.

Trust and the Therapeutic Relationship

As noted above, difficulty with trust appears to be an occupational hazard for law enforcement officers, who typically maintain a strong sense of self-sufficiency and insistence on solving their own problems. Mental health clinicians, who work with police officers, may at first need get past some testing and questioning on the part of their patients: "Why are you doing this?" "What's in it for you?" "Who's going to get this information?" Officers may expose the therapist to mocking cynicism and criticism about the job, baiting the therapist to agree, and thereby hoping to expose the therapist's prejudices about law enforcement culture and practices (Silva, 1991; Wester & Lyubelsky, 2005).

The development of trust during the establishment of the therapeutic alliance depends on the therapist's skill in interpreting the officer's statements, thoughts, feelings, reactions, and nonverbal behavior. In the best case, the officer begins to feel at ease with the therapist and finds comfort and a sense of predictability from the psychotherapy process. Silva (1991) articulates several guidelines for establishing therapeutic mutual trust:

Accurate empathy. The therapist conveys his or her understanding of the officer's background and experience (but beware of premature false familiarity and phony "bonding").

Genuineness. The therapist is spontaneous, yet tactful, flexible and creative, and communicates as directly and non-defensively as possible.

Availability. The therapist is accessible and available (within reason) when needed, and avoids making promises and commitments he or she can't realistically keep.

Respect. This is both gracious and firm, and acknowledges the officer's sense of autonomy, control, responsibility, and self-respect within the therapeutic relationship. Respect is manifested by the therapist's overall attitude, language, and behavior, as well as by certain specific actions. These include signifying regard for rank or job role by initially using formal departmental titles, such as "officer," "detective," or "lieutenant," at least until trust and mutual respect allow an easing of formality. Here it is important for clinicians to avoid the dual traps of patronizing and talking down to the officer on the one hand, and, on the other hand, trying to "play cop" or force bogus camaraderie by assuming the role of a colleague or supervisor.

Concreteness. Therapy should, at least initially, be goal-oriented and have a problem-solving focus. Police officers are into action and results, and to the extent that it is clinically realistic, the therapeutic approach should emphasize active problem-solving approaches before exploring more sensitive and complex psychological issues (Brooks, 1998; Wester & Lyubelsky, 2005).

Therapeutic Strategies and Techniques

In general, the effectiveness of any therapeutic strategy will be determined by the timeliness, tone, style, and intent of the intervention. Effective psychological interventions with law enforcement officers share in common the following elements (Blau, 1994; Fullerton et al, 1992; Miller, 1995, 1998d, 2000a, 2000b, 2006*l*, in press-c; Wester & Lyubelsky, 2005):

Briefness. Utilize only as much therapeutic contact as necessary to address the present problem. The officer does not want to become a "professional patient."

Limited focus. Related to the above, the goal is not to solve all the officer's problems, but to assist in re-stabilization from the critical incident and provide stress-inoculation for future incidents.

Directness. Therapeutic efforts are directed to resolve the current conflict or problem to reach a satisfactory short-term conclusion, while planning for the future, if necessary.

Interestingly, reminiscent of Violanti's (1999) conceptualization of police work as "civilian combat," a very similar intervention model has recently been articulated by military psychologist and U.S. Army Captain Bret Moore for dealing with soldiers experiencing combat stress (Munsey, 2006). The program goes under the acronym, BICEPS, which stands for:

Brevity. Treatment is short, addressing the problem at hand.

Immediacy. Intervention takes place quickly, before symptoms worsen (recall secondary and tertiary prevention from Chapter 1).

Centrality. Psychological treatment is set apart from medical facilities, as a way to reduce the stigma soldiers might feel about seeking mental health services (although it could be argued that putting mental health treatment in a special category might make some soldiers feel alienated from their colleagues who've suffered "real" injuries).

Expectancy. A soldier experiencing problems with combat stress is expected to return to duty (this positive expectancy is consistent with the METTLE model).

Proximity. Soldiers are treated as close to their units as possible and are not evacuated from the area of operations.

Simplicity. Besides therapy, the basics of a good meal, hot shower, and a comfortable place to sleep, ensure a soldier's basic physical needs are met.

Blau (1994) recommends that the first meeting between the therapist and the law enforcement officer establish a safe and comfortable working atmosphere. This is fostered by the therapist's articulating a positive endorsement of the officer's decision to seek assistance, a clear description of the therapist's responsibilities and limitations with respect to confidentiality and privilege (Miller, 2006*l*), and an invitation to the officer to state his or her concerns.

A straightforward, goal-directed, problem-solving therapeutic intervention approach includes the following elements (Blau, 1994):

Create a sanctuary. The officer should feel safe that what he or she says will be used only for the purposes of his or her healing and strengthening. Indeed, once the initial wariness passes, many officers report that they actually find the clinician's office a refuge from departmental politics and shop talk, a place where they can be "real."

Focus on critical areas of concern. Mental Toughness-oriented therapy should be goal-directed and focused on resolving specific adaptation and recovery issues related to the crisis at hand, which is a corollary of the next principle.

Specify desired outcomes. Not: "I'd like to feel more at ease with my work and my family," But: "I want to reduce the number of intrusive thoughts about the call to a level where I can ride patrol with my partner and pay attention to the neighborhood." And: "I'd like to be able to step back for a few seconds to regain control before I blow up at my wife and kids over nothing." Not that the officer will typically come in with pre-set concrete goals of this type; indeed, officers are often initially confused about what they hope to accomplish. In the early phases, it is primarily the clinician's task to help the officer sort out, focus, and operationalize his or her goals so that there will be a way of measuring if the therapy process is accomplishing them.

Develop a general plan. Remember *satisficing* from Chapter 2? Apply this to the therapeutic process to be able to begin effective intervention from the first session. Develop an initial game plan that can be modified as you go along. All the details needn't be worked out at this point and the plan will be revised as new information comes in: 20/20/20. But you have to start somewhere, so develop a general road map that will allow you to—

Identify practical initial implementations. Begin intervention as soon as possible. This induces confidence quickly as well as allowing the therapist to get feedback from treatment efforts thus far that will guide further interventions, again: 20/20/20. In line with enhancing confidence and motivational change is the general philosophy of METTLE interventions—

Review assets and encourage self-efficacy. Consistent with the overarching aim of Mental Toughness psychotherapy as a strengthening, not weakening, process, it is as important to know what personal strengths and resources the officer has, as it is to understand his or her vulnerabilities. In primary, secondary, and tertiary prevention and intervention, we always capitalize on strengths to overcome or work around weaknesses.

Blau (1994) delineates a number of effective individual intervention strategies for police officers:

Attentive listening. This includes good eye contact, appropriate body language, genuine interest, and interpersonal engagement, without inappropriate comment or interruption. Clinicians will recognize this type of intervention as a form of "active listening (Miller, 2006*l*)."

Being there with empathy. This therapeutic attitude conveys availability, concern, and awareness of the disruptive emotions being experienced by the traumatized or distressed officer. It is also helpful to let the officer know, in a non-alarming manner, what he or she is likely to experience in the days and weeks ahead.

Reassurance. In acute stress situations, this should take the form of realistically reassuring the officer that routine matters will be taken care of, deferred responsibilities will be handled by others, and that the officer has administrative and command support. This, of course, should be realistically based.

Supportive counseling. This includes active listening, restatement of content, clarification of feelings, and validation. It also may include such concrete services as community referral and networking with liaison agencies, if necessary.

Interpretive counseling. This type of intervention should be used when the officer's emotional reaction is significantly greater than the circumstances of the critical incident seem to warrant. In appropriate cases, this therapeutic strategy can stimulate the officer to explore underlying emotional or psychodynamic issues that may be intensifying a naturally stressful traumatic event (Horowitz, 1986). In a few cases, this may lead to continuing, ongoing psychotherapy.

Not to be neglected is the use of *humor,* which has its place in many forms of psychotherapy (Fry & Salameh, 1987), but may be especially useful in working with law enforcement and emergency services personnel (Fullerton et al, 1992; Henry, 2004; Miller, 1995, 1998d, 2006*l*; Silva, 1991). In general, if the therapist and patient can share a laugh, this may lead to the sharing of more intimate feelings. Humor serves to bring a sense of balance, perspective, and clarity to a world that seems to have been warped and polluted by malevolence and horror. "Show me a man who knows what's funny," Mark Twain said, "and I'll show you a man who knows what's not."

Humor, even sarcastic, gross, or callous humor, if handled appropriately and used constructively, may allow the venting of anger, frustration, resentment, or sadness, and thereby lead to productive, reintegrative therapeutic work. This is true, however, only insofar as the therapist is able to keep a lid on destructive types of self-mockery or inappropriate projective hostility in the form of sleazy, cynical, or mean-spirited sniping or character assassination.

Also remember that many traumatized individuals tend to be quite concrete and suspicious at the outset of therapy, and certain well-intentioned kidding and cajoling may be perceived as insulting to the officer or dismissive of the seriousness of his plight. In such cases, the constructive therapeutic use of humor may have to await the formation of a therapeutic relationship that allows some cognitive and emotional breathing room, as well as the reclaiming of enough of the officer's confidence and self-esteem so that he can take some perspective on the situation and "lighten up." Some extreme events, however, such as the death of a child or fellow officer, may never be funny—*ever*—and this has to be respected.

Utilizing Cognitive Defenses

In psychology, *defense mechanisms* are the mental stratagems the mind uses to protect itself from unpleasant thoughts, feelings, impulses, and memories. While the normal use of such defenses enables the average person to avoid conflict and ambiguity and maintain some consistency to their personality and belief system, most psychologists would agree that an overuse of defenses to wall off too much unpleasant thought and feeling leads to a rigid and dysfunctional approach to coping with life. Accordingly, much of the ordinary psychotherapeutic process involves carefully helping the patient to relinquish pathological defenses so that he or she can learn to deal with internal conflicts more constructively.

However, in the face of immediately traumatizing critical incidents, the last thing the affected person needs is to have his or her defenses stripped away. If you sustain a broken leg on the battlefield, the medic doesn't stop to clean the wound, put you under anesthesia, set the bone, wrap you in a cast, and nurse you back to health. Hell, no: he binds and braces the limb as best and as fast as he can—with a dirty tree branch and fishing line if necessary—and helps you hobble out of there, double-time.

In the same way, for an acute psychological trauma, the proper utilization of psychological defenses can serve as an important "psychological splint" or "emotional field dressing" that enables the person to function in the immediate posttraumatic aftermath and eventually be able to productively resolve and integrate the traumatic experience when the luxury of therapeutic time can be afforded (Janik, 1991). Think of this set of strategies as the post-incident counterpart to the pre-incident and mid-incident cognitive strategies described in Chapter 6.

In their regular daily work or in critical incidents, law enforcement and public safety personnel usually need little help in applying defense mechanisms on their own. Examples (Durham et al, 1985; Henry, 2004; Taylor et al, 1983) include:

Denial. "Put it out of my mind; focus on other things; avoid situations or people who remind me of it."

Rationalization. "I had no choice; things happens for a reason; it could have been worse; other people have it worse; most people would react the way I'm doing."

Displacement/projection. "It was Command's fault for issuing such a stupid order; I didn't have the right backup; they're all trying to blame me for everything."

Refocus on positive attributes. "Hey, this was a one-shot deal—I'm usually a great marksman; I'm not gonna let this jam me up."

Refocus on positive behaviors. "Okay, I'm gonna get more training, increase my knowledge and skill so I'll never be caught with my pants down like this again."

Janik (1991) proposes that, in the short term, clinicians actively support and bolster psychological defenses that temporarily enable the officer to continue functioning. Just as a physical crutch is an essential part of orthopedic rehabilitation when our leg-injured patient is learning to walk again, a psychological crutch is perfectly adaptive and productive if it enables the officer to get back on his emotional two feet as soon as possible after a traumatic critical incident. Only later, when he or she is making the bumpy transition back to normal life, are potentially maladaptive defenses revisited as possible impediments to progress.

And just as some orthopedic patients may always need one or another kind of assistive walking device, like a special shoe or a cane, some degree of psychological defensiveness may persist in officers so they can otherwise productively pursue their work and life tasks. Indeed, rare among us is the person who is completely defense-free. Only when defenses are used inappropriately and for too long—past the point where we should be walking on our own psychological two feet—do they constitute a "crutch" in the pejorative sense.

Survival Resource Training

As noted in Chapter 8, a recently evolving trend in trauma psychotherapy emphasizes the importance of accessing and bolstering the patient's natural powers of resilience, and the constructive marshalling of strength and resistance to stress and disability (Calhoun & Tedeschi, 1999; Dunning, 1999; Miller, 1998a, 1998d; Stuhlmiller & Dunning, 2000; Tedeschi & Calhoun 1995; Tedeschi & Kilmer, 2005; Violanti, 2000). In this vein, Roger Solomon (1988, 1991) has been ahead of the curve in capitalizing on the idea that constructive denial of vulnerability and mortality can be an adaptive response for law enforcement officers coping with ongoing critical incidents and their immediate aftermath.

Solomon (1988, 1991) points out that, following critical incidents characterized by fear, danger, injury, or death, officers often dwell on their mistakes and overlook what they *did right* in terms of coping with their emotions and getting the job done.

Thus, being realistically reminded by the clinician of their own adaptive coping efforts may prove especially empowering because it draws upon strengths that come from the officer him- or herself. Termed *survival resource training,* this intervention allows officers to utilize the fear response to tap into a state of controlled strength, increased awareness, confidence, and clarity of mind.

In this technique, the clinician encourages the officer to view the critical incident from a detached, objective point of view, "like you were watching a movie of yourself," and to go through the incident "frame-by-frame." At the point where he images himself fully engaging in this activity (negotiating, arresting, taking cover, firing his weapon, etc.), the officer is instructed to "focus on the part of you enabling you to respond." Note that this process can be enhanced by mastering the arousal, attention, imagery, and cognitive techniques described in Chapters 3–6 of this book.

In most cases, the survival resource training procedure leads to a mental reframe characterized by controlled strength, heightened awareness, confidence, and mental clarity, as the officer mentally zooms in on his capability to respond, instead of focusing on the immobilizing fear, perceptions of weakness, loss of control, or perceptual distortions. Often, this results in officer's being "reminded" of how he put his fear on hold and rose to the occasion in order to get the job done. The reframing thus focuses on resiliency instead of vulnerability, strength instead of weakness.

In addition to processing past critical incidents, realistic feelings of efficacy and competence can also shade over into future incidents, as officers have reported increased confidence and ability to handle subsequent calls, such as arrests, shooting incidents, domestic disturbances, and traffic chases. In addition, officers have felt more confident in other non-emergency but stressful situations, such as court testimony, and personal matters, such as resolving family conflicts (Miller, 2006h, 2007; Solomon, 1988). It is especially gratifying to clinicians and officers alike when their mutual efforts can turn vicious cycles of demoralization and despair into positive cycles of confidence and optimism. Indeed, this is the hoped-for outcome of all forms of psychotherapy (Miller, 1993a, 1998d, 2006*l*).

Finding Meaning In Adversity: "Existential Toughness"

Recall from Chapter 9's discussion of group debriefing models that trying to force-feed a "positive meaning" or "life lesson" from a noxious experience can be counterproductive: some bad things in life just plain suck and no amount of philosophical sugar-coating is going to make a turdball taste like a jelly donut. But human beings are meaning-making creatures, and people will naturally grope to find reasons or messages hidden in even the most grotesque catastrophes. When this comes from the officer him- or herself, it must be respected and nurtured in the psychotherapy process because a consolidation of one's worldview is, in itself, a resiliency-enhancing—i.e. mental toughening— process.

In general, existential treatment strategies that focus on a quest for meaning, rather than just alleviation of symptoms, may productively channel the worldview conflicts generated by the traumatic event. This may include helping the officer to formulate an acceptable "survivor mission" or "professional purpose" (Henry, 2004; Shalev et al, 1993). In the best cases, as we saw in Chapter 8, the rift and subsequent reintegration of the personality may lead to an expanded self-concept, a renewed sense of purpose, and a new level of psychological, spiritual, and career growth (Bonanno, 2005; Calhoun & Tedeschi, 1999; Tedeschi & Calhoun, 1995, 2004; Tedeschi & Kilmer, 2005). Of course, not all trauma victims, law enforcement officers included, are able to achieve this successful reintegration of their ordeal and many struggle with at least some vestige of emotional injury for a long time, perhaps for life (Everstine & Everstine, 1993; Matsakis, 1994; McCann & Pearlman, 1990; Miller, 1998d).

Therefore, my main caution about these transformational therapeutic conceptualizations is that they be presented as an opportunity, not an obligation. The extraction of meaning from adversity is something that must ultimately come from the officer him- or herself, not be foisted upon him or her by the clinician. Such existential "forced conversions" are often motivated by a need to reinforce the clinician's own meaning system, or they may be part of what I call a therapeutic "Clarence-the-Angel fantasy" (Miller, 1998d), wherein the enlightened clinician swoops down and, by dint of the therapist's brilliantly insightful ministrations, rescues the hapless patient from his or her darkest hour.

Realistically, as mental health clinicians, we can hardly expect all or even most of our traumatized patients to miraculously transform their tragedy and acquire a fresh, revitalized, George Bailyean outlook on life—how many of *us* would respond that well? But, as noted above, human beings do crave meaning (Yalom, 1980) and if a philosophical or religious orientation can nourish the officer in his or her journey back to the land of the living, then the therapeutic role must sometimes stretch to include some measure of guidance in affairs of the spirit.

Organizational and Departmental Support

Not all interventions involve psychotherapy or debriefings. Following a department-wide critical incident, such as a line-of-duty death, serial homicide investigation, or mass casualty rescue and recovery operation, the departmental psychologist or consulting mental health professional can advise and guide law enforcement agencies in encouraging and implementing several *organizational response measures* (Alexander, 1993; Alexander & Walker, 1994; Alexander & Wells, 1991; DeAngelis, 1995; Fullerton et al, 1992; Palmer, 1983). Many of these strategies are proactively applicable as part of training before a critical incident occurs. Others apply even when there is no specific incident, but just involve cops in a jam seeking support and relief (Miller, 1995, 2006*l*). Some specific organizational and leadership measures include the following:

> *Encourage mutual support among peers and supervisors.*
> The former typically occurs anyway; the latter may need some explicit reinforcement. Although not typically

team workers like firefighters or paramedics, police officers frequently work as partners and understand that
some degree of shared decision-making and mutual reassurance can enhance effective performance on the job, as
well as helping to deal with tragedy.

*Utilize humor as a coping mechanism to facilitate emo-
tional insulation and group bonding.* The first forestalls
excessive identification with victims, the second encourages mutual group support via a shared language. Of
course, as noted earlier, mental health clinicians and departmental supervisors need to carefully monitor the line
between adaptive humor that encourages healing and
gratuitous nastiness that only serves to entrench cynicism and despair.

*Make use of appropriate rituals that give meaning and
dignity to an otherwise existentially disorienting experience.* This includes not only religious rites related to
mourning, but such respectful protocols as a military-
style honor guard to attend bodies before disposition,
and the formal acknowledgement of actions above and
beyond the call of duty.

Make productive use of grief leadership. This involves
the commanding officer demonstrating by example that
it's okay to express grief and mourn the death of fallen
comrades or civilians, and that the dignified expression
of one's feelings about the tragedy will be supported, not
denigrated. Indeed, this healthy combination of master-
ful task-orientation and validated expression of legitimate grief has largely characterized the response of
rescue and recovery personnel at the New York World
Trade Center and other mass-casualty disaster sites
(Henry, 2004; Regehr & Bober, 2004).

*Show respect for psychological issues and psychological
services.* If the departmental brass doesn't believe that
encouraging the appropriate utilization of psychological
services is a valid way of expressing their concern and

support for their troops' welfare, then the rank and file won't buy it, either. Psychological referrals should be de-stigmatized and supported as a health and safety measure, the same as with medical referrals and general fitness maintenance.

In summary, the mental health interventions following a critical incident described in Part III of this book supplement and support the pre-incident training described in Part II. In total, these comprise the primary, secondary, and tertiary prevention measures of the METTLE model. Officers who deal best with critical incidents prepare their minds and bodies proactively through rigorous training and avail themselves of legitimate support services during and after a critical incident. In this way, they become tough, act tough, and stay tough, while retaining the mental agility, flexibility, and humanity that are necessary for top-notch law enforcement work.

PART IV:

Special Applications of METTLE

11

Peril on Patrol:
Survival is Your Job

The Role of Patrol in Policing

When most people think of police officers, they think of the beat cop or squad car team, and indeed, the police patrol function continues to be the backbone of community law enforcement (Peak, 2003, Peak & Glensor, 2002, Toch & Grant, 2005). This seemingly simple police activity is really composed of a variety of complex daily decisions and activities. These include the discretionary use of authority and prevention of criminal activity by an assertive police presence. It also involves maintaining good relations with citizens in the community, because, like it or not, officers may at times have to depend on those citizens to help them do their jobs effectively; for example, obtaining useful information in trying to solve a crime, or helping to maintain order and calm neighbors' anger to forestall a potential civil disturbance. If nothing else, officers know they will encounter the same people—"repeat customers"—on a regular basis, and so maintaining good relations works in everybody's favor (Miller, 2006*l*; Russell & Beigel, 1990; Toch & Grant, 2005).

While the actual effect of foot and vehicle patrol officers on crime statistics is still being debated, surveys clearly show that citizens feel safer and more confident in their local police department when the officers are a living, breathing presence in the daily life of their communities. Ironically, however, it is the neighborhood patrols that are often the first to undergo budget cuts in favor of more flashy special tactics and investigative units (Thibault et al, 2004).

141

For patrol cops to do their jobs effectively, they must adopt a constructive territoriality about their patrol areas, sometimes known as *owning the beat* (Peak, 2003). By becoming increasingly familiar with the geography, economy, personality, and sociology of their beats, patrol cops come to know intuitively what's normal or what's out of place for their respective neighborhoods. Additionally, by adopting the optimal blend of professional detachment and emotional involvement in their neighborhoods, patrol officers develop what the business world calls *buy-in,* a personal stake in the welfare of their patrol community, a situation in which it is important to them to keep the peace and provide the highest quality of service: "This is my neighborhood, and I'm going to do everything I can to make sure that it stays safe."

Relatedly, officers who feel they are an integral part of their communities are less likely to resort to physical force to resolve crisis situations that could be nonviolently de-escalated. In return, citizens come to trust and respect those officers they perceive as consistently trying to keep order without excessive harshness, and who truly try to understand the community's concerns (Toch & Grant, 2005; Wadman & Zinman, 1993). Thus, this is truly one aspect of policing that exemplifies the principle that the best form of crisis intervention is crisis prevention (Chapter 1). And being able to manage daily stress and handle critical incidents is a vital part of this process.

Elements of Effective Patrol Policing

Survey research (Baehr et al, 1968; Peak, 2003) has identified a number of tasks and responsibilities that patrol officers must carry out in order to successfully perform their patrol duties. Although TV cop shows often portray police work as nonstop action, in real life the patrol officer's job is more like that of a firefighter, paramedic, or air traffic controller: long periods of monotony punctuated by brief episodes of intensity. Officers have to be able to react quickly and go from "0-to-60" at a moment's notice. They have to be able to respond courageously and aggressively in critical situations, yet possess sufficient presence of mind not to overreact and risk inflaming the situation further. In between, they must deal with various and sundry crises, ranging from citizen disputes to traffic violations.

To be effective, officers have to gain intimate knowledge of their patrol areas: the geography, economy, demographics, crime statistics, local culture and quirky characters on their beats. Only in this way will they hone their instincts as to what's normal and what's suspicious in their patrol areas. This practical expertise further enables officers to quickly size up situations and make prompt, effective decisions with regard to what specific actions to take, such as a crime in progress, family crisis, or citizen dispute: a practical application of *recognition-primed decision-making* (RPDM), discussed in Chapter 2.

While not all officers can be Olympic athletes, they are expected to maintain some basic standards of physical conditioning and psychomotor skill with respect to strength and endurance, manual dexterity, facility with firearms and equipment, driving skill, and so on. In the same way, while not all officers can be paragons of psychological health and virtue, all cops are expected to have the basic mental skills of mature judgment, problem-solving, and independent thinking. Indeed, even more so than other emergency responders, police officers are given wide latitude in how to handle many types of routine and complex policing situations, ranging from the decision to write a traffic ticket, to whether to use their taser or firearm in a dangerous criminal confrontation. In this regard, police officers need to be able to work under varying levels of supervision; from tight micromanagement of their every move to almost no supervision at all, leaving important decisions to the officer's judgment and discretion (Blau, 1994; Miller, 2006*l*).

Important psychological skills extend to the interpersonal domain as well. Patrol officers, especially in larger metropolitan areas, will have to deal with a wide range of citizen ages, ethnicities, cultures, economic strata, personalities, and psychopathologies. Officers must often endure impolite or verbally abusive behavior, while maintaining a professional presence at all times, and carefully treading the line between authori*tative* (think Sheriff Andy Taylor) and authori*tarian* (think Deputy

Barney Fife) police presence. Effective officers must be able to utilize appropriate conflict-resolution skills to prevent situations from escalating, while maintaining objectivity, balance, and the perception of fairness. They must be able to cope with different kinds and varying degrees of stress, and yet at all times maintain a high level of personal integrity and ethical conduct. This is not just a nice, politically correct idea; it is essential to maintaining authority and credibility on patrol (Miller, 2006*l*; Peak, 2003, Peak & Glensor, 2002; Thibault et al, 2004).

In all of these activities, and especially when it comes to dealing with potentially dangerous situations or critical emergencies, the METTLE process can help officers fine-tune their perceptions and reactions for maximal effectiveness on patrol.

Applications of METTLE to Patrol Policing

In his comprehensive manual on street survival tactics, Garner (2005) lays out the essential guidelines for patrol officers' survival on the streets, which I have here grouped into four categories, along with applications of the METTLE model.

Prepare for the Encounter

Preparation is both general and specific. *General preparation* includes all the facets of an officer's training, maintaining growing proficiency through continued practice, developing what this book has characterized as true *expertise* (Chapter 2). It also includes basic personal maintenance, i.e. staying in decent physical shape. Being a master exponent of 37 different styles of martial arts won't do you much good if you get winded in the first 37 seconds of combat.

Specific preparation involves learning as much about a specific impending encounter as possible before jumping in. On patrol, you often won't be afforded the luxury of prolonged planning and preparation time: events have a way of unfolding real fast. But even if you are abruptly summoned to the scene of a domestic dispute or robbery in progress, or you turn the corner and come across an attempted sexual assault or drug deal, there are usually at least a few precious seconds to engage your

METTLE skills to scope out the scene and mentally suit up for the encounter. This leads to the next set of guidelines.

Assess the Situation

Again, only rarely will you have to act ballistically and just bolt into a situation, pushing a child out of the path of a speeding car, for example. In most patrol situations, you can stop, look, and listen, taking advantage of the opportunity to marshal your METTLE skills of arousal, attention, imagery, and thought management to prepare for the upcoming encounter. Use your multisensory and multidirectional scanning skills (Chapter 4) to gather as much information as possible about the scene you're poised to enter. Your psychological radar and experienced-based expertise will make you especially sensitive to subtle danger signs that a less well-trained officer might miss. For example, a usually noisy restaurant may be too quiet, suggesting a hold-up in progress.

One other benefit of careful observation and analysis is to self-examine whether you and your partner are up to the task in terms of both numbers and range of expertise. You might be able to handle a simple family spat or disperse a few unruly teens, but what if you are called to the scene of a domestic disturbance and it turns out to be a complex family violence/hostage-barricade situation? Or upon closer observation of the teenage crowd, it appears that their behavior is drawing the attention and involvement of onlookers and the situation threatens to escalate into a gang battle or civil disturbance? At these times, it's important to know when to call for backup before intervening on your own. Once you're in the thick of trouble, it may be too late to summon assistance, so being proactive is usually best. You can invoke your imagery skills (Chapter 5) to internally rehearse several scenarios for handling the type of scene you're about to enter.

Enter the Scene

Now you're in it. You've committed yourself to some course of action and you must achieve control of the situation as quickly as possible. Even on your way into the site, always be conscious of your approach and positioning with respect to others—seen and unseen—who might be in the vicinity. Observe everything: people, the surrounding environment, opportunities for cover, routes of escape. Use your scanning ability to take in and analyze the situation in its entirety. Always be cognizant of your own position with respect to potential threats around you. Don't make unwarranted assumptions about people or circumstances; when in doubt, exercise caution. Never relax your vigilance or take any unknown situation for granted: keep looking for more. That means don't rush in if you don't have to; "cowboy" tactics are rarely effective in controlling a potentially dangerous scene and may result in injury to yourself or your partners.

Use cover and concealment appropriately. With a two-officer team, Garner (2005) recommends utilizing *contact and cover*. The *contact officer* enters the scene and carries out the main business of the encounter: mediating a citizen dispute, dispersing a crowd, writing a summons, searching a vehicle, making an arrest, and so on. Meanwhile, the *cover officer* hangs back and observes the contact officer's interaction, ready to call for backup and spring into action with all necessary force if the situation demands it. Partners should work out a set of subtle verbal and nonverbal communication signals to cue each other during an encounter with a suspect (Burns, 2006; Davis, 2005). These can be adaptations of the self-cuing techniques described in Chapter 6. The key is to rehearse and practice them until they become automatic, i.e. the RPDM principle (Chapter 2).

When interacting with a subject, maintain your caution and vigilance. Be courteous and authoritative, non-demeaning but no-nonsense. Maintain a *reactionary gap* of 5–6 feet separating you from the subject, just enough distance to react and defend yourself, or close in and restrain the subject if necessary. While talking to the subject, use your diffuse attentional scanning beams to take in what's going on around you, while allocating at least one focused attention beam on the subject's hands at all times (Chapter 4). Be ready for surprises—that way, you'll be less likely to overreact if something occurs abruptly.

As an example, Garner (2005) recommends the following protocol for approaching an unknown, suspicious subject; note that these steps are perfectly adaptable to the METTLE model.

First, as you begin your approach, scan the environment for potential cover possibilities: you don't know who's going to jump out of where and what they're going to do. Identify yourself: "Police officer. I'd like to talk to you for a minute, please."

Once you've made contact, maintain the 5–6 foot reactionary gap and don't let the subject close in on you: "Please remain right where you are, sir. Thank you." Never stand between two subjects or let anyone maneuver behind you. If possible, keep the subject facing away from you while you call for backup.

Always watch the subject's hands. If his hands are in his pockets, don't order him to remove them until you are ready to react. Then say, "Very, very slowly, I want you to take your hands out of your pockets and I want your hands to be completely empty. Put your hands where I can see them." If he does anything suspicious, you may have to draw your weapon and seek cover. Always be safe and err on the side of caution. Remember to be courteous but firm and no-nonsense about your instructions. If you determine that it is not necessary to take the subject into custody, make your break with him a clean one: "Okay, sir, you're free to go. I appreciate your cooperation and have a nice day." Keep your eyes on him until you and he are at a safe distance.

In all phases of your encounter, utilize arousal control techniques (Chapter 3) to keep yourself from either being too relaxed or too tensed—either extreme will make you less efficient at observing, analyzing, and responding to the scene as needed.

Control the Scene

In the majority of routine patrol activities, your interventions will not involve arrest or actual use of force. Most patrol situations can be managed nonviolently and even many arrests are carried out without undue danger to officer or subject. However, there will be circumstances when you must control the scene to keep things from escalating and many of these situations will require you to assert the full range of your police authority.

As noted earlier, while some situations may permit an extended period of planning, too much preparation can bog down into stalling and procrastination, and Garner (2005) urges that, at some point, the responding officer *make a decision.* The decision does not have to be a perfect one, just one that helps the situation. In this context, it is useful to recall the RPDM principle from Chapter 2: that a decision that *satisfices* and basically controls and stabilizes the crisis in the here-and-now is better than a painstakingly crafted perfect strategy that is formulated too late to do any good (Haughton, 2005; Spaulding, 2005). Remember, what makes RPDM effective is the background of training, practice and experience that underlies it. Based on this informed assessment, whatever you determine is the right thing to do right now that will help the situation—do it.

If your activity primarily involves the search of a building, vehicle, or individual suspect, make sure you search thoroughly and correctly, as many times as you feel is necessary to make the situation safe. While you search, be continually aware of what's going on in your environment. Use your attentional scanning skills to keep alert to changes in illumination, sounds, movement, or anything else. Also use this sensory analysis to know when to make a tactical retreat if the odds are against you or if the situation intuitively just doesn't feel right. Use your professional common sense, which is really another way of saying your experience-based RPDM. If you must exert necessary force, recall the psychological survival skills of Chapter 7 to summon the resolve of the winning mindset and *know* you will be the victor in this encounter.

Recover from the Incident

Use cognitive restructuring, self-talk, and other thought and language techniques (Chapter 6) to mentally debrief yourself following the incident. Remember the 20/20/20 hindsight/insight/foresight rule (Chapter 1) and utilize it to your advantage to turn every incident into a training module.

This goes for your emotional state as well. A severe encounter can't help but leave an emotional after-trace, and if you're having difficulty processing it, get the appropriate assistance in the form of a group or individual stress debriefing or individual counseling (Chapters 9 and 10). Remember, you're responsible for taking care of your master control station—your brain.

METTLE Skills in Vehicle Stops and Searches

One of the most common patrol police scenarios is the traffic stop. Indeed, most citizens who come in contact with a police officer will do so in the context of a traffic ticket or accident. But even the most routine encounter can become a potentially deadly *high-risk vehicle stop.* Or you might be actively investigating or pursuing known or suspected felons in a vehicle and can expect trouble when you attempt to pull them over. Accordingly, Garner (2005) makes a number of essential recommendations for such encounters, to which officers can apply the METTLE skills learned in this book. Obviously, you will tailor your specific approach to the needs of each situation.

Evaluate and Prepare

As with any patrol action, prior to engaging the vehicle and its occupants, try to learn as much as possible about who you may be dealing with. Run the plates. Contact dispatch for updated info. Call for backup. Discuss with your partner and/or backup officers possible plans and scenarios for handling the scene. Use imagery and cognitive self-cuing strategies (Chapters 5 and 6) to mentally rehearse and verbally work out practical strategies you may use in various scenarios that may unfold.

Pullover and Initial Confrontation

Use your operational training, METTLE skills, and common sense. At night, always try to make the stop in a well-lighted area. Even better, try to maneuver the stop so that the suspect is in bright light and you are mostly obscured (the *"him-in-the-*

light-me-in-the-dark" principle). Never pull up alongside or in front of the subject's vehicle, but keep your vehicle to the rear of the subject, preferably in his right-side blind spot.

When the vehicles have come to a complete stop, find available cover, draw your weapon if necessary, and have one officer clearly issue the instruction: "Police! Put your hands on your head!" If the subjects don't immediately comply, repeat the instruction. When the occupants finally comply, continue: "Driver, remove your keys and drop them out the window. Now put your hands back on your head." Maintain vigilance at all times. This is where your METTLE skills of arousal and attentional control will come into play, as you maintain the OAL (optimal arousal level) and appropriate beams of attention to modulate your own physiological reactivity and keep track of what's going on around you (Chapters 3 and 4).

Control the Scene

The next phase is bringing the subjects out of the vehicle. Remember your operational training and have a flexible plan worked out with your partner and/or backups. With officers safely positioned, begin bringing out the car's occupants, one at a time: "Driver, reach outside with your left hand and open the car door. Step out slowly and step away from the car. Face the front of your car and freeze. Do not turn towards us."

Have your partner and/or backups continue to cover any remaining vehicle occupants. Instruct the driver to walk slowly to a point between your vehicle and the backup's vehicle and tell the subject: "Go down on your knees. Keep your hands on your head. Keep looking straight ahead. Don't look back at us. Cross your ankles. Stay in that position and don't move." Have your partner or backup handcuff the subject, pat him down for weapons or other dangerous objects (e.g. needles), and bring him to a waiting police car. Remember the rule about searching as often as you feel the need. Repeat this process for the other vehicle occupants. All officers should always remain vigilant for any sign of resistance from the subject or suspicious activity from the vehicle or surrounding environment.

If a weapon or other direct threat to officer safety is spotted during the search, the officer who discovers it should immediately shout a warning to his peers. The next warning is to the weapon's owner: "We see the weapon. If you touch it, you will be shot." Or, if the weapon is in the subject's hand: "Put down the weapon slowly. Do it now or you will be shot." Then, follow your operational training with regard to weapon control and neutralization.

Even when all the known occupants of the vehicle are in custody, this is still not the time to let down your guard. How do you know there's not another suspect hiding on the floor of the van? In the trunk of the sedan? Underneath the vehicle? In the bushes? It's happened before. Garner (2005) recommends that, even if you're not sure if anyone else is in or around the vehicle, it's better to be safe than sorry: "You, hiding in the vehicle—sit up with your hands on your head immediately!" If you get no response, repeat the challenge. If you still get nothing, especially if the other suspects swear there's no one there, one backup officer moves quietly up on the left side of the suspect's car under cover of the other officers. The interior of the passenger compartment is cleared first, followed by the trunk and any other conceivable hiding place. At all times, your attentional beams should be scanning the environment for additional threats.

Bam! You're jumped from behind by a guy who, it later turns out, leaped out of the vehicle early and was hiding in those bushes. If that happens, give him the Chapter 7 treatment: defend your life, take him down, use only as much force as necessary to win the encounter, but if it unavoidably comes down to a choice of who goes home tonight, make sure it's you.

Finally, when the situation has been safely resolved, utilize your METTLE arousal control, self-talk, and cognitive restructuring techniques (Chapters 3 and 6) to tone down the adrenalin rush and congratulate yourself for a job carried out with safety, efficiency, and integrity.

12

Officer-Involved Shooting I: In the Danger Zone

The gun.

As a law enforcement officer, you are unique among civilian public safety and emergency service personnel in that no other nonmilitary professional group is mandated to carry a lethal firearm as part of their daily gear, nor charged with the responsibility to use their own discretion and judgment in making split-second decisions as to whether to use deadly force and take a human life in the line of duty. Watching any typical TV cop show might convince the viewer that most officers blithely pop off rounds at perps without a second thought. In reality, the firing of one's weapon in the line of duty is a profound event that almost always leaves a psychological trace and, in some cases, may be traumatic enough to end a career in law enforcement (Miller, 2006k, 2006*l*; Solomon, 1990; Solomon & Horn, 1986).

Cop and Guns: Facts and Stats

Statistics indicate that about six hundred criminals are killed each year by police officers in the United States. Some of these killings are in self-defense, some are accidental, and others are done to prevent harm to citizens. By comparison, about 135 officers are killed in the line of duty each year. When you consider the ratios in the general population, proportionately far more cops are killed by civilians each year than the other way around. In most cases, an officer's taking a life occurs in the context of trying to save a life. Not surprisingly, confronting and shooting an armed perpetrator is universally regarded by police officers as one of the most stressful aspects of their job (Anshel et al, 1997; Gudjonsson & Adlam, 1985; Miller, 2006k; Sewell, 1983; Violanti & Aron, 1995).

The sources of stress attached to such an *officer-involved shooting* (OIS) are multiple, and include the officer's own psychological reaction to taking a life; the responses of law enforcement peers and the officer's family; rigorous examination by departmental investigators and administrators; possible criminal and civil court action; attention and sometimes harassment by the media and "crusading reporters"; and possible disciplinary action or change of assignment (Baruth, 1986; Blau, 1994; Miller, 2006k; Russell & Beigel, 1990).

In most jurisdictions, the legal test for justification of legitimate use of lethal force by police officers requires that any reasonable person with the training and experience of the involved officer would have perceived a lethal threat in the actions taken by the suspect (Blum, 2000). Line-of-duty deadly force actions are most likely to occur in the following situations, in roughly descending order of probability: (1) domestic or other disturbance calls; (2) robbery in progress; (3) burglary in progress; (4) traffic offense; (5) personal dispute and/or accident; and (6) stake-out and drug bust (Blau, 1994; Rodgers, 2006; Russell & Beigel, 1990).

Of American police officers who kill a suspect in the line of duty, 70% are out of law enforcement within five years (Horn, 1991). Some authorities believe the psychological disability rate from OIS's, and from critical incidents in general, has been overestimated (Curran, 2003). According to McMains (1986a, 1991), by the early 1980s, an estimated 95% of police officers involved in a line-of-duty shooting had left police work within five years. By the mid-1980s, large departments had cut that rate to 3%, while smaller departments were still losing about two-thirds of officers involved in a shooting. The important difference seems to be in the level of administrative and mental health support provided to officers by the larger departments, either because of broader philosophies or broader budgets, giving their officers the clear message that helping them resolve the trauma and maintain their mental health is a departmental priority.

Officer-involved Shooting: Perceptual, Cognitive, and Behavioral Disturbances

Most officers who have been involved in a deadly force shooting episode have described one or more alterations in perception, thinking, and behavior that occurred during the event (Artwohl, 2002; Duran, 1999; Honig & Roland, 1998; Honig & Sultan, 2004; Miller, 2006k, 2006*l*; Solomon & Horn, 1986; Wittrup, 1986). Most of these can be interpreted as natural adaptive defensive reactions of an organism under extreme emergency stress.

Most common are *distortions in time perception*. In the majority of these cases, officers recall the shooting event as occurring in slow motion, as if in the slo-mo segment of an action movie or sports broadcast. In this state, officers may describe being aware of numerous details they would have overlooked if the perception were happening in real-time. This phenomenon may represent the brain increasing its own processing speed to allow the individual to take in as much survival data as quickly as possible in a brief span of time. A smaller percentage of officers report experiencing the event as speeded up.

Sensory-perceptual distortions are common and most commonly involve *tunnel vision,* in which the officer is sharply focused on one particular aspect of the visual field—typically, the suspect's weapon—while blocking out everything in the periphery. More generally, this is sometimes referred to as the *weapon focus effect* (Hulse & Memon, 2006; Kavanaugh, 2006; Loftus et al. 1987; Pickel, 1998, 1999; Steblay, 1992), in which crime victims or witnesses have been found to focus their attention on the weapon to the exclusion of everything else around them. For victims and witnesses, this usually presents a problem in recalling important details of the crime, such as the perpetrator's face and what actions he took. When it happens to police officers, this constricted beam of attention means that the officer may neglect to scan the environment for additional threats that may be looming in the environment, placing him or her in danger of surprise attack (Chapters 4 and 7).

Similarly, *tunnel hearing* may occur, in which the officer's auditory attention is focused exclusively on a particular set of sounds, most commonly the suspect's voice, while background sounds are excluded. Sounds may also seem muffled or, in a smaller number of cases, louder than normal. Officers have reported not hearing their own or other officers' gunshots. In a few cases, officers have reported hearing "the bad guy's blood drip" (James Sewell, personal communication). Overall perceptual clarity may increase or diminish.

Because the human mind is complex, the relationship among different cognitive phenomena in a critical situation can also be complex. Speed-accuracy trade-offs and restrictions in range of perception are common in emergency situations. Behaviorally, decision makers under stressed conditions tend to lose flexibility, become rigid in their responding, and rely on familiar responses that are not necessarily appropriate to the immediate situation, or they may perseverate in those patterns long after they have ceased to be useful (Gigerenzer, 1991; Janis & Mann, 1977; Kavanaugh, 2006; Staw et al, 1981).

One recent study (Hulse & Memon, 2006) found that, when police officers were presented with several types of simulated critical incident scenarios, officers recalled far fewer details of an event that was more emotionally arousing, such as a shooting scenario, than those of an event that was less arousing, i.e. a domestic dispute incident. However, although the high-arousal condition led to recall of fewer details, those details were recalled with far more accuracy than in the low-arousal condition. This kind of narrowing and sharpening of perceptual focus under stress is related to the subject of cognitive style discussed in Chapter 4 and, again, argues for practical training in both arousal and attentional control techniques (Chapters 3 and 4).

Some form of *perceptual and/or behavioral dissociation* may occur during the emergency event. In extreme cases, officers may describe feeling as though they were standing outside or hovering above the scene, observing it "like it was happening to someone else." In milder cases, the officer may report that he or she "just went on automatic," performing whatever actions he or she took with a sense of robotic detachment. As noted in Chapter 2, going on automatic is not necessarily a bad thing if it represents an expression of well-practiced RPDM strategies. Some officers report intrusive distracting thoughts during the scene, often involving loved ones or other personal matters, but it is not known if these substantially affected the officers' actions during the event.

Disturbances in memory are commonly reported in shooting cases. About half of these involve impaired recall for at least some of the events during the shooting scene; the other half involve impaired recall for at least part of the officer's own actions—this may be associated with the "going-on-automatic" response discussed above. More rarely, some aspects of the scene may be recalled with unusually vivid crystal clarity—a *flashbulb memory.* Over a third of cases involve not so much a loss of recall as a distortion of memory, to the extent that the officer's account of what happened differs markedly from the report of other observers at the scene. For example, it is common for officers not to remember the number of rounds fired, especially from a semiauto handgun.

Some cases of recall distortion can be described as *tunnel memory,* where some part of the scene is recalled especially vividly, while others are fuzzy or distorted (Hulse & Memon, 2006; Safer et al, 1998). As with research on eyewitness memory in general (Loftus et al, 1989), one's subjective vividness of the recall is often uncorrelated with the accuracy of the material recalled; that is, one can be very certain of what he or she thinks happened, and still be dead wrong.

Perception, time distortion and memory are all related, of course. You may not remember something later because you weren't paying attention to it in the first place. And, because the mind abhors loose ends, when trying to construct a coherent recollection of what really went down, there is a tendency to confabulate—to fill in the mental blanks with our best guess of what actually took place; this, of course, is one of the banes of attorneys who deal with eyewitness testimony (Loftus et al,

1989). One administrative implication of these kinds of cognitive distortions is that discrepant accounts among participants in, and eyewitnesses to, a shooting scene should not be automatically interpreted as any of these persons lying or consciously distorting his report (Artwohl, 2002), but may well represent honest differences of perception and recall.

A general neuropsychological explanation for these constrictions of sensation, perception, and memory is that the brain naturally tries to tone down the hyperarousal that occurs during a critical shooting incident, so that the individual can get through the experience intact, using his or her mental autopilot responses. In a smaller number of cases, heightened perceptual awareness occurs to those features of the scene that are essential for the officer's survival. And the processing of accurate memories for later use seems to take a neuropsychological back seat to the mechanisms necessary for getting the officer through the situation alive, right here and now (Miller, 1990, 1998d, 2006k). The implications for training are that a greater depth, range, and flexibility of attention and arousal control will allow officers to use such automatic responding adaptively in a wider range of extreme situations, topics covered in Chapters 3 and 4.

A *sense of surprise, disbelief, and/or helplessness* may occur during a shooting episode, but may be under-reported due to the potential embarrassment and stigma attached (Duran, 1999; Honig & Sultan, 2004). A very small proportion of officers report that they "froze" at some point during the event: either this is an uncommon response or officers are understandably reluctant to report it. In a series of interviews, Artwohl (2002) found that most of these cases represented the normal *action-reaction gap* in which officers make the call to shoot only after the suspect has engaged in clearly threatening behavior. In most cases, this brief evaluation interval is a positive precaution, to prevent the premature shooting of a harmless citizen. But in cases where the prudent action led to a tragic outcome, this appropriate hesitation may well be viewed retrospectively as a fault: "If I hadn't waited to see him draw, maybe my partner would still be alive."

Much more common, in my experience, is the opposite phenomenon, a sense of relief, particularly in officers who have been involved in their first OIS: "I wish I didn't have to shoot the guy in the first place, but I'm glad to know that, when it came down to it, I was able to do what had to be done."

Applying the METTLE Approach to Officer-involved Shootings

Again, it's all about the training. The bottom line is to train proactively in as many realistic simulated scenarios as possible in order to make your responses automatic—"by instinct"— when a real-life scenario presents itself. This is, after all, the whole rationale behind developing the skills for naturalistic, recognition-primed decision-making (RPDM) discussed in Chapter 2, which is exactly the kind of cut-to-the-chase, rapid-response decision-making required for emergency situations like OISs. For example, the International Association of Chiefs of Police (IACP) reports that approximately 90% of police shootings take place within a three-second period (Kavanaugh, 2006), far too short a time to stand there and weigh options in a logical, trial-and-error format.

Duran (1999) describes a technique for breaking out of tunnel vision during a critical incident which relies on the straightforward behavioral strategy of *deliberate eye movement.* Fixating on a restricted visual field is, after all, both a perceptual and a behavioral response, so enlisting your eye muscles to help widen the field seems like a natural strategy. In fact, there is a neurophysiological basis for this (Miller, 1990, 1993). Visual perception is decoded primarily in the brain's occipital lobe (at the rear of the brain) while voluntary eye movements are mediated by the *frontal eye fields* of the brain's frontal lobes. These two brain regions have reciprocal connections and work in tandem, so that what we see is determined by where we point our eyes, and where we next direct our gaze is guided by what we've just seen, and so on. So, if you're visually fixated on a particular object or scene—e.g. the perp's gun barrel—to the exclusion of other information that might be of potential importance—e.g. another bad guy sneaking up behind you—then it's probably in your best interest to do something to break the hyperfocused perceptual spell.

To counteract the tunnel vision effect, Duran (1999) recommends deliberately moving your head and eyes from side to side. Obviously, you still need to pay attention to the danger in front of you, so I recommend you combine this strategy with the multiple-beams-of-focus technique described in Chapter 4. That is, keep one concentrated attentional beam steadfastly on the immediate threat, while scanning the environment with another, more diffused beam of attention—remember the flashlight analogy—and use the eye and head movements to reinforce this.

Of course, there's a limit to how many simultaneous beams of focus you can keep going at one time, and you may have to rapidly oscillate back and forth between scanning broadly and zooming in. But if you've practiced the attention-focusing strategies in Chapter 4, you should almost automatically be able to adjust your perceptual aperture to the appropriate field of focus. At the same time, you'll probably be using the arousal-control techniques of Chapter 3 to keep your attention and arousal in sync—not too high, not too low, but just right for the situation at hand.

Remember, too, that awareness of your environment is multisensory. While you're focusing on the danger in front of you and visually scanning the environment for additional threats, you should also be *listening* to what's going on around you (Duran, 1999). If you've practiced utilizing multisensory beams of attention (Chapter 4) and if you've internally rehearsed multiple simulated shooting scenarios in imagery (Chapter 5) and in real-life simulation training, and if you can constructively use positive thoughts and cues phrases (Chapter 6) to talk yourself through tight spots, you'll be as mentally prepared to handle the OIS or any other crisis situation as you can possibly be.

Cue phrases and self-talk may have special application to OIS situations because of the need for rapid, coordinated, and perfectly timed motor skills and behavioral sequences. Under stress, manual dexterity and other fine motor skills can break down (Duran, 1999). To minimize this, it is important to have trained and practiced with these skills, using imagery and self-cuing

(Chapters 5 and 6), and also in real-life training scenarios. At the same time, because OISs are naturally high-adrenalin situations, incorporate attention and arousal control strategies in your training (Chapters 3 and 4) to keep your psychophysiological state on an even keel. Finally, be prepared to evoke your critical survival skills training (Chapter 7) if you feel you're in danger of being overwhelmed. For an OIS, as much as for any other incident in police work, remember the ITTS rule and use it.

13

Officer-Involved Shooting II: Surviving the Aftermath

If you've fired your weapon in the line of duty, you know that the crisis isn't over when the bad guy has been neutralized and the response team has arrived at the scene. Depending on how the incident turned out, you may experience a variety of reactions in the hours, days, weeks, or longer, following an OIS. By employing the secondary and tertiary principles of the METTLE program, you'll be much better able to handle the challenges ahead.

Psychological Reactions of Officers to an Officer-involved Shooting

The etiology of many post-shooting reactions lies in the emotional disconnect between most officers' expectations about a heroic, armed confrontation and the actual reality of most shooting scenarios, which typically involve petty criminals, mentally disordered suspects, suicide-by-cop scenarios, or accidents (Blau, 1986, 1994; Miller, 2006b, 2006k; Rodgers, 2006; Russell & Biegel, 1990).

OIS Reaction Typologies

Although the reaction to an OIS will necessarily be influenced by the individual personality and experiences of the officer, several analyses (Anderson et al, 1995; Blau, 1994; Blum, 2000; Nielsen, 1986) have suggested three general typologies of post-shooting reaction, which parallel the three types of reaction noted to occur in the wake of traumatically stressful events in general (Bowman, 1997; Miller, 1998d; see also Chapter 8). These, of course, should be thought of as a continuum, not as discrete categories. In addition to individual officer characteristics, the severity of a post-shooting reaction will be determined by a host of situational factors, such as the nature of the shooting itself, the post-incident investigation, reactions of brass, peers, and family, and so on. Each of these reaction types also has its own therapeutic implications for helping officers in distress, as will be discussed further below.

The first type of reaction involves a transitory period of post-incident psychological distress, which the officer is able to resolve within a few weeks, largely by self-coping efforts, such as talking with colleagues and family, praying and reflecting, and reexamining and renewing life priorities and goals. The psychological distress does not appear to substantially affect the officer's daily functioning. Peer counseling, a CISD debriefing (Chapter 9), and perhaps one or two visits with a mental health professional or clergyperson, is usually all the intervention that's required.

The second type of reaction is somewhat more intense, with post-traumatic symptoms persisting for several weeks or months (Chapter 8). The officer's daily functioning may be impaired, often with a "good days/bad days" pattern. In addition to peer support and group debriefings, short-term crisis counseling with a psychologist (Chapter 10) may be indicated to help the officer work through the traumatic elements of the shooting, as well as to provide support through any contentious administrative processes that may follow the incident.

The third type of reaction is characterized by severe psychological disability, what officers often describe as a "breakdown" or "meltdown." The shooting incident has so traumatized the officer that he is unable to function or he becomes a discipline problem or an otherwise dysfunctional employee (Miller, 2004a, 2006e, 2006f, 2006g). In most cases, this kind of severe reaction occurs in the context of some degree of vulnerability in the premorbid personality of the officer, often exacerbated by a particularly adversarial investigation and perceived lack of support from colleagues, the department, family, and/or the community. Treatment will necessarily involve more long-term psychotherapy, perhaps with medication. Although some of these officers will ultimately leave police work, many of these careers may be salvaged by timely and appropriate psychological intervention (Miller, 1998d, 2000a, 2006k, 2006*l*).

OIS Reaction Phases

Some authorities (Nielsen, 1986; Williams, 1999) have divided the post-shooting reaction into several basic stages or phases, starting with an *immediate reaction* or *impact phase*. For officers who have just shot a suspect during a dangerous confrontation, there may be an initial reaction of relief and even exhilaration at having survived the encounter.

Later, feelings of guilt or self-recrimination may surface, especially where the decision to shoot was less clear-cut or where the suspect's actions essentially forced the hand of the officer into using deadly force, such as in botched robberies, domestic disputes, hostage-barricade scenarios, or suicide-by-cop incidents (Miller, 2005e, 2006b, 2006k). Or the officer may simply be faced with the fact that, however justified his response, he has nevertheless taken a human life or injured another human being. During this *recoil* or *remorse phase,* the officer may seem detached and preoccupied, spacily going through the motions of his job duties, and operating on autopilot. He may be sensitive and prickly to even well-meaning questions and attaboys by his peers ("Way to go, Bobby—you got the scumbag!"), and especially to accusatory-like interrogation and second-guessing from official investigators or the press ("Officer Jackson, did you really fear for your life and believe you had no choice but to fire on that teenager?").

As the officer begins to come to terms with the shooting episode, a *resolution* or *acceptance phase* may be seen, wherein he or she comes to grips with the fact that his actions were necessary and justified in the battle for survival that often characterizes law enforcement deadly encounters (Chapter 7). This process may be complicated by persisting departmental investigations or by impending or ongoing civil litigation (Miller,

2006e, 2006h). In addition, even under the best of circumstances, resolution may be partial rather than total, and psychological remnants of the experience may continue to haunt the
officer periodically, especially during future times of crisis. But
overall, he is eventually able to return to work with a reasonably
restored sense of confidence.

In the worst case, sufficient resolution may never occur, and
the officer enters into a prolonged *post-traumatic phase,* which
may effectively end his or her law enforcement career. In less
severe cases, a period of temporary stress disability allows the
officer to seek treatment, eventually regain his or her emotional
and professional bearings, and ultimately return to the job. Still
other officers return to work right away, but perform marginally
or dysfunctionally until their actions are brought to the attention of superiors (Miller, 2004a, 2006f, 2006g).

In my experience, most officers who have been traumatized
by their own use of deadly force can be effectively returned to
work with the proper psychological intervention and departmental support (Miller, 1995, 1998d, 2006k, 2006*l*). Indeed, this
very support from above is typically what prompts the referral
for mental health counseling in the first place.

Types of Post-Shooting Symptoms and Reactions

Again, the officer's individual personality and experience will
influence the type of post-shooting reaction he or she experiences, but certain commonalities of reactions emerge from various reports (Anderson et al, 1995; Blum, 2000; Cohen, 1980;
Geller, 1982; Honig & Sultan, 2004; Rodgers, 2006; Russell &
Beigel, 1990; Williams, 1999). Some of these will represent general post-traumatic reactions familiar from Chapter 8, while others will be more specific to an OIS.

Physical symptoms may include headaches, stomach upset,
nausea, fatigue, muscle tension and twitches, and changes in
appetite and sexual functioning. Sleep is typically impaired,
with frequent awakenings and possibly nightmares. Post-traumatic reactions of intrusive imagery and flashbacks may occur,
along with premonitions, distorted memories, and feelings of
déjà vu. Some degree of anxiety and depression is common,

sometimes accompanied by periodic panic attacks. There may be unnatural and disorienting feelings of helplessness, fearfulness, and vulnerability, along with self-second-guessing and guilt feelings. Substance abuse may be an additional risk (Miller, 2005c, 2006*l*).

There may be a pervasive irritability and low frustration tolerance, along with anger and resentment toward the suspect, the department, unsupportive peers and family, or civilians in general. Part of this may be a reaction to the conscious or unconscious sense of vulnerability that the officer experiences after a shooting incident. Sometimes, this is projected outward as a smoldering irritability that makes the officer's every interaction a grating source of stress and conflict. All this, combined with an increased hypervigilance and hypersensitivity to threats of all kinds, may result in over aggressive policing, leading to abuse-of-force complaints (Garner, 1995; Geller & Toch, 1996; Miller, 2004a, 2006f, 2006g).

Ultimately, this may spiral into a vicious cycle of angry and fearful isolation and withdrawal by the officer, spurring further alienation from potential sources of help and support. At the same time, some officers become overly protective of their families, generating an alternating *control-alienation syndrome* (Williams, 1999)—clinging to and micromanaging them one moment, pushing them away the next—which is disturbing and disorienting to family members (Miller, 2007). All this, combined with cognitive symptoms of impaired concentration and memory, may lead the officer to fear that he or she is "going crazy."

Officer-involved Shooting: On-scene Response

All of the factors noted above have important implications for productive departmental management and helpful clinical intervention of OISs at every stage of the event. As noted throughout this book, the METTLE model seeks to capitalize on natural and healthy social support from comrades and supervisors as a vital element in bolstering mental toughness. So to begin with, every officer who has risked his life should be treated with basic respect. Even if there is a suspicion of misconduct (Miller, 2004a, 2006e, 2006f, 2006g), there is nothing to be gained from an adversarial attitude; indeed, an officer who is treated decently will be more inclined to cooperate with investigators. Thus, the proper handling of involved officers begins at the shooting scene itself and the following recommendations are addressed primarily to law enforcement supervisors and the mental health clinicians who advise them.

OIS On-Scene Law Enforcement Response

In many departments, an OIS results in the call-out of many departmental personnel, including backup officers, the involved officer's supervisors, the Chief of Police or Sheriff in some jurisdictions, paramedics, and typically the department psychologist, if there is one. One composite model protocol for on-scene response to officer-involved shootings (Baruth, 1986; Blau, 1994; IACP, 2004; McMains, 1986a, 1986b, 1991; Williams, 1991) is presented here as an operational expression of the METTLE model. This protocol should, of course, be adapted and modified to the particular needs of your individual police agency. As an application of secondary prevention (Chapter 1), how this protocol is carried out in practice can make a tremendous difference in the officer's later psychological adjustment and reinforcement of resilience and mental toughness.

At the scene, reassurance to the involved officer should be provided by departmental authorities. "Reassurance" doesn't have to (and at this early stage, probably shouldn't) entail any value judgment about the officer's actions, but should simply communicate an understanding and appreciation of what the officer has just experienced, and the assurance that the department will support him or her as much as possible throughout the process.

The officer should be provided on-scene access to legal counsel and a mental health professional. In many jurisdictions officers may refrain from making any statements to authorities at the scene until an attorney is present and/or until they have been assessed as mentally fit to make such a statement by a qualified mental health professional. On the one hand, this protects the officer's rights and at the same time assures that any statements made cannot later easily be challenged as having been made under duress (Cloherty, 2004; Miller, 1998d, 2006h, 2006*l*).

The officer's weapon will almost always be impounded. In the best case, the weapon is turned over in private, with an attitude of respect, and in many cases a replacement weapon is provided or the empty holster removed while the on-scene investigation proceeds. Following the walk-through, it is recommended that the officer be removed from the scene as quickly as possible and that nobody hang around at the scene longer than necessary. If possible, the officer should be driven home or back to the station by two colleagues, to await further action. If taken home, they should accompany him to his door and leave only when he has assured them he is okay. The officer's family should be notified of the shooting, in person and as soon as possible, even if personnel are still on-scene: the last thing you want is for the family to hear about the shooting on the radio or TV, or get a call from a neighbor who's seen or heard the story.

If media arrive at the scene, the officer should be shielded from them and any statements should be made through a departmental spokesperson. Most medium-to-large size departments have a Public Information Officer (PIO) who is part of the critical response team. In general, any statement that could affect the internal investigation or other legal action should be avoided and every effort should be made to discourage a carnival atmosphere. Agencies should consult with their attorneys about local and state regulations in these areas as part of the process of developing their own policies for OISs.

OIS On-Scene Psychological Intervention

If you are a police psychologist who responds to OIS scenes, this section is addressed to you. As part of the on-scene response team, you have a specific but important role to play (Blau, 1994; McMains, 1986a, 1986b, 1991; Miller, 2006k, 2006*l*).

First, determine the nature of the incident. When you get the call, try to find out as much as possible about the incident and the current scene. This may vary, depending on the timing of the call. Sometimes, you may get called within minutes of the shooting incident, in which case there's not much info to be had, other than the location of the scene (sometimes, as I've learned the hard way, even this can be iffy). At the other extreme, you may be called almost as an afterthought, long after the rest of the responders have arrived at the scene, only because an unforeseen emotional complication occurs and the bulb goes on in somebody's head: "Hey, don't we have a psychologist who's supposed to handle these things?" This kind of oversight usually represents a problem with the call-out policy at the planning stages or it may occur in a very dangerous or complex scene where tactical and/or medical services legitimately take precedence. As a rule, however, if there is a call-out psychologist, he or she should be summoned to the scene as early as possible, even if he or she must wait around to do something useful.

As the responding psychologist, when you arrive at the site, first check in with the scene commander and then locate the involved officer(s) and determine their psychological status. This may range from the extremes of panic, confusion, and disorientation—rare, in my experience—to unnatural calmness and stoic denial ("I'm okay; no problem"), a far more common response. Sometimes, emotions will swing back and forth at the scene, the officer blank and icy one moment, then nervous and shaky the next. As discussed below, validating these reactions as normal stress responses is an important part of on-scene intervention.

Try to find a comfortable place to conduct your interview with the officer. "On-scene" doesn't necessarily have to mean standing over the body or pacing back and forth in front of the news cameras. I've conducted on-scene interviews behind bushes, under trees, behind a throng of officers or a row of vehicles, in the back seat of patrol cars, and in a SWAT wagon. As long as the officer stays inside the established perimeter and can be found by authorities when needed, he or she is still technically on-scene. If you have any doubts, check with the scene commander.

For the visibly upset officer, you may have to use calming and distraction techniques to bring his mental state into a more rational and receptive mode. For the defensive, sealed-over officer, what often proves helpful is a version of the CISD procedure (Chapter 9), condensed into a three-phase, one-on-one model, called a *defusing* (Mitchell & Evely, 1996, 2003):

First, ask the officer to tell you what happened. This will typically elicit a stiff, dry, detail-laden rendition of events, as if the officer were testifying before a review board or a courtroom:

> *Officer:* I saw the guy coming out the dark breezeway, carrying a box or something bulky like that, hugging the wall like he was trying to hide. I identified myself as a police officer and told him to stop, put the box down slowly, and face the wall. He dropped the box and put his hand in his pocket. I drew my weapon and ordered him to freeze. He pulled out something metal, which I took to be a blade or a firearm. I drew down on him in a Weaver stance and ordered him to drop the object. He raised it higher and started coming towards me. In fear for my life, I fired, I think, three or four times. He fell and was quiet, and the object skidded several feet away into the grass. I radioed for backup and attempted to administer aid, but I think he was already dead. I located the object and found that it was a butterfly knife with the blade out.

Listen to the story until you have a good sense of the sequence of events. Next, ask the officer to describe "what was going on in your mind while it was happening." This often elicits clues to the officer's cognitive and emotional state:

> *Officer:* The guy and me kind of surprised each other. I guess neither of us expected the other one to be on the campus that time of night, so we both sort of jumped when we saw each other. I could feel the adrenalin jack up my body. I don't think I really had time to be nervous,

I just kind of went on automatic and the whole thing had a kind of unreal feeling to it—like it was me doing it, but it wasn't me. After I found the knife and called on the radio, that's when it hit me I could've been killed if I waited a second longer to fire. Then, shit, suddenly I'm shaking like a little girl; it was embarrassing. But I pulled it together before the other guys got there.

Finally, provide information and support regarding any disturbing reactions the officer may be having at the scene. Remember that the goal of on-scene psychological intervention is not to perform in-depth psychotherapy—that may be needed later or it may not. For now, you want to allow the officer to loosen up just enough for you to be able to assess his mental status, but you want to encourage him to use whatever mental toughness techniques he already knows to help him keep his head together until the immediate crisis is resolved:

Psychologist: Hey, your brain and your body are just following the textbook. Any time somebody's in an emergency or crisis mode, human nature puts us on autopilot so we know just enough of what to do so we can live through the experience. It's like the adrenalin acts like mental Novocain to numb you out just enough to survive and let your survival instinct and training kick in. Then, after this "Novocain" wears off, you feel all the emotions in an exaggerated way, like a rebound effect or a delayed reaction. So, from what you're telling me, there's nothing unusual about your response. It's not my ultimate judgment call to make, but from how you described it, it sounds like you did what you felt you had to do.

As noted above, one reason for an accurate assessment of the officer's mental status at the scene is the determination of mental fitness to make a statement to authorities, which may be very important for subsequent legal aspects of the case. Although in my experience this is rare, some officers may be sufficiently confused, disoriented, emotionally vulnerable, and cognitively suggestible to be legally incompetent to understand their legal rights and/or to make a statement to authorities at the scene—a kind of "temporary insanity" caused by extreme traumatic stress. In such cases, the psychologist may recommend that investigators wait until the officer has had a chance to recover some measure of psychological equilibrium, which may require only a few minutes to calm down and some basic reassurance at the scene, or, in the extreme case, may necessitate removal to a safe facility for further evaluation and treatment.

Following the on-scene evaluation, and while still at the site, the psychologist should make a recommendation for a follow-up evaluation at his or her office, scheduled several days post-incident. This gives the officer a little time to chill out and loosen up, and allows the clinician to get a better perspective on how the officer is coping psychologically after the initial shock of the incident has worn off. This also serves as an informal fitness-for-duty evaluation in a nonconfrontational setting; additionally, such an FFD evaluation may be formally mandated by some departments as a precondition of the officer returning to work (Miller, 2006e, 2006*l*; Rostow & Davis, 2004). In general, if you assess the officer to be experiencing no unusual signs or symptoms (some degree of residual distress is normal for a few days or weeks), you will probably recommend release to full duty. Otherwise, you may make a range of recommendations, such as more time off with subsequent follow-up or continued psychotherapy. Again, police psychologists should always consult with their departments regarding protocols for such incidents—ideally, they should be involved in developing those protocols in the first place.

Psychological Intervention for Officer-involved Shootings

Following the original shooting incident and the follow-up session, some officers may require or request additional sessions with the psychologist "to get my head straight about this." In other cases, there may not have been any on-scene intervention at all, and the follow-up consultation is the first contact between the officer and the psychologist. In the meantime, there may or may not have been a CISD or other group procedure (Chapter 9). As with any critical incident, it is important that each department have in place a system for smooth and non-stigmatized referral of officers for mental health counseling when they need it. The following recommendations are again addressed to the law enforcement mental health clinician.

Principles and Guidelines of Post-Shooting Intervention

McMains (1986a, 1991), Somodevilla (1986), and Wittrup (1986) have developed a set of recommendations for implementing psychological services following an OIS, which have been adapted here for incorporation into the tertiary prevention phase of the METTLE program. The reader will note that many of these are in fact specialized applications of the general principles of law enforcement critical incident intervention discussed in Chapters 9 and 10.

The intervention should begin as soon after the shooting incident as possible, even, as noted above, on-scene. In some cases, an officer's obvious distress at the scene or shortly thereafter creates the need for an immediate intervention. In other cases, distress may be suppressed or concealed for hours, days, or weeks, so intervention must await the time that the problems in coping become apparent. In such cases, intervention should not be rushed, but should be started as quickly as possible when the need surfaces. In any event, a departmental policy should be developed that gives priority to these referrals, so that at a minimum, an officer can be seen within 24 hours of a request.

To provide for the most efficient and effective use of time and resources, subsequent intervention should be undertaken at a location that the officer finds safe and non-threatening, usually an office away from the department. In most cases, this will be the clinician's office. Depending on the officer's shift schedule, a regular time should be established for the sessions.

Consistent with the METTLE model of resilience-strengthening, psychological intervention should be short-term and focused on supporting officers through the crisis, as well as returning them to active duty as soon as possible. How narrow or broad the range of issues to be covered will be determined on a case-by-case basis, depending on how the incident has affected the officer, his family, his colleagues, and others. But the general guideline is that post-shooting psychological intervention should be focused on resolving the critical incident in question and re-establishing and reinforcing adaptive mental toughness.

Post-shooting investigations can be contentious. Clinically, the psychologist should remember that his or her role in these treatment settings is as therapist and supportive advocate, not investigator or judge. What you are advocating for is the officer's mental health and stability, not any particular side of the case. Accordingly, a realistically positive atmosphere should prevail during the course of the intervention. Absent any clear evidence to the contrary, the assumption should be that the officer acted properly, can successfully manage the current crisis, and will soon return to active duty. Indeed, during particularly ugly investigations, the clinical consulting room may be the only place the officer does not feel like a hounded suspect. Accordingly, every effort must be made to insure doctor-patient confidentiality. Any unavoidable breaches of that confidentiality, such as FFD reports and disability determinations, should be anticipated and discussed in advance (Miller, 1998d, 2004a, 2006e, 2006k, 2006*l*).

Post-Shooting Psychotherapeutic Strategies

On initial contact with the officer, the psychologist's role may replicate the basic intervention stages of the CISD model (Chapter 9): First, review the facts of the case with the officer. Similar to the fact phase of a CISD, this allows for a relatively non-emotional narrative of the traumatic event. But in the case of an OIS, it serves a further function. Precisely because of the cognitive and perceptual distortions that commonly occur in these kinds of incidents (Chapter 12), what may be particularly disturbing to the officer is the lack of clarity in his own mind as to what really happened. Just being able to review what is known about the facts of the case in a relatively safe and non-adversarial environment may provide a needed dose of mental clarity and sanity to the situation. If the officer seems "stuck" in expressing the narrative, employ the *frame-by-frame technique* (Solomon, 1988, 1991), described in Chapter 10.

Next, review the officer's thoughts and feelings about the shooting incident. This resembles the thought and reaction phases of a CISD, but may not be as cut-and-dried as with a typical group debriefing. Remember, an OIS represents a special kind of critical incident and it may take more than one go-round for the officer to productively untangle and reveal what's going on in his mind. Give him extra time or extra sessions to express his thoughts and feelings, and be sure to monitor the reaction so as not to encourage unproductive spewing or loss of control. One of the most important things the psychologist can do at this stage is to help modulate emotional expression so that it comes as a relief, not as an added burden. To facilitate this, the clinician can guide the officer in the use of the arousal-control techniques described in Chapter 3.

Provide authoritative and factual information about psychological reactions to a shooting incident. The kinds of cognitive and perceptual distortions that take place during an OIS, the post-traumatic symptoms and disturbances, and the sometimes off-putting and distressing reactions of colleagues and family members, are likely to be alien to the officer's ordinary experience and might be interpreted by him or her as signs of going soft or crazy. Normalize these responses for the officer, taking a somewhat more personal and individualistic approach than might be found in the typical group CISD information/education phase. Often, just this kind of authoritative reassurance from a credible mental health professional can cut officer's anxiety considerably. One area where the clinician may be especially helpful is in introducing and instructing the officer in many of the mental toughness exercises described in Chapters 3–6.

Finally, provide for follow-up services which may include additional individual sessions, family therapy, referral to support services, possible medication consult, and so on. As with most cases of critical incident psychological intervention, follow-up psychotherapy for OISs tends to be short-term, although additional services may be sought later for other personal, family, or professional problems that are only partially related or even unrelated to the current incident (Miller, 1998d, 2006*l*, 2007). Indeed, any kind of critical incident may often be the stimulus to explore other troublesome aspects of an officer's life, and the success in resolving the incident with the psychologist may give the officer confidence to pursue these other issues in an atmosphere of trust.

CONCLUSION

Mental Toughness and Mental Health

You now understand that *mental toughness* means flexibility, resilience, and decisiveness of action. Like any skill worth knowing, the METTLE concepts and techniques you've learned in this book should be reinforced through ongoing training and practice—remember: ITTS. Keep at it and you'll gradually weave together your own individual style of psychological body armor. You may actually surprise yourself at how much better you're managing daily stresses and handling critical emergencies more smoothly and competently. Most importantly, I hope this book has given you a glimpse of the potentially powerful relationship that psychology and law enforcement can forge together in developing and enhancing the tools officers use to do their jobs safely, competently, and honorably.

And, as I stated in the Introduction, I welcome your feedback; please feel free to contact me with your comments and suggestions on how to make subsequent editions of this book and my training courses better—ITTS goes for me, too.

Thank you all for your service and stay safe.

—LM

BIBLIOGRAPHY

Alba, J.W. & Hutchinson, J.W. (1987). Dimensions of consumer expertise. *Journal of Consumer Research, 13,* 411–454.

Alexander, D.A. (1993). Stress among body handlers. A long-term follow-up. *British Journal of Psychiatry, 163,* 806–808.

Alexander, D.A. & Walker, L.G. (1994). A study of methods used by Scottish police officers to cope with work-related stress. *Stress Medicine, 10,* 131–138.

Alexander, D.A. & Wells, A. (1991). Reactions of police officers to body-handling after a major disaster: A before-and-after comparison. *British Journal of Psychiatry, 159,* 547–555.

Alexander, F. (1950). *Psychosomatic medicine: Its principles and applications.* New York: Norton.

Almedom, A.M. (2005). Resilience, hardiness, sense of coherence, and post-traumatic growth: All paths leading to "light at the end of the tunnel," *Journal of Loss and Trauma, 10,* 253–265.

American Psychiatric Association (1980). *Diagnostic and statistical manual of mental disorders* (3rd ed.). Washington DC: American Psychiatric Association.

American Psychiatric Association (2000). *Diagnostic and statistical manual of mental disorders* (4th ed., text revision). Washington DC: American Psychiatric Association.

Anderson, W., Swenson, D. & Clay, D. (1995). *Stress management for law enforcement officers.* Englewood Cliffs: Prentice Hall.

Annett, J. (1995). Motor imagery: Perception of action: *Neuropsychologia, 33, 33* 1395–1417.

Annett, J. (1996). On knowing how to do things: A theory of motor imagery. *Cognitive Brain Research, 3,* 65–69.

Anshel, M., Robertson, M. & Caputi, P. (1997). Sources of acute stress and their appraisals and reappraisals among Australian police as a function of previous existence. *Journal of Occupational and Organizational Psychology, 70,* 337–356.

Antonovsky, A. (1987). *Unraveling the mystery of health: How people manage stress and stay well.* San Francisco: Jossey-Bass.

Artwohl, A. (2002). Perceptual and memory distortion during officer-involved shootings. *FBI Law Enforcement Bulletin,* October, pp. 18–24.

Asken, M.J. (1993). *PsycheResponse: Psychological skills for optimal performance by emergency responders.* Englewood Cliffs: Regents/ Prentice Hall.

Baehr, M.E., Furcon, J.E. & Froemel, E.C. (1968). *Psychological assessment of patrolmen: Qualifications in relation to field performance.* Washington DC: Department of Justice.

Band, S.R. & Vasquez, I.J. (1999). The will to survive. In L. Territo & J.D. Sewell (Eds.), *Stress management in law enforcement* (pp. 297–302). Durham: Carolina Academic Press.

Bandura, A. (1977). Self-efficacy: Toward a unifying theory of behavioral change. *Psychological Review, 84,* 191–215.

Bandura, A. (1986). *Social foundation of thought and action: A social cognitive theory.* Englewood Cliffs: Prentice-Hall.

Baruth, C. (1986). Pre-critical incident involvement by psychologists. In J.T. Reese & H.A. Goldstein (Eds.), *Psychological services for law enforcement* (pp. 413–417). Washington DC: USGPO.

Bernard, C. (1865). *Introduction a l'etude de la medecine experimentale.* Paris: Bailliere et Fils.

Behncke, L. (2006). Mental skills training for sport: A brief review. *Athletic Insight: The Online Journal of Sport Psychology,* www.athleticinsight.com.

Bisson, J.I. & Deahl, M.P. (1994). Psychological debriefing and prevention of post-traumatic stress: More research is needed. *British Journal of Psychiatry, 165,* 717–720.

Blau, T.H. (1986). Deadly force: Psychological factors and objective evaluation—A preliminary effort. In J.T. Reese & H.A. Goldstein (Eds.), *Psychological services for law enforcement* (pp. 315–334). Washington DC: USGPO.

Blau, T.H. (1994). *Psychological services for law enforcement.* New York: Wiley.

Blum, L.N. (2000). *Force under pressure: How cops live and why they die.* New York: Lantern Books.

Bohl, N.K. (1991). The effectiveness of brief psychological interventions in police officers after critical incidents. In J.T. Reese, J.M. Horn & C. Dunning (Eds.), *Critical incidents in policing* (pp. 31–38). Washington DC: US Department of Justice.

Bohl, N. (1995). Professionally administered critical incident debriefing for police officers. In M.I. Kunke & E.M. Scrivner (Eds.), *Police psychology into the 21st century* (pp. 169–188). Hillsdale: Erlbaum.

Bonanno, G.A. (2005). Resilience in the face of potential trauma. *Current Directions in Psychological Science, 14,* 135–138.

Bordow, S. & Porritt, D. (1979). An experimental evaluation of crisis intervention. *Psychological Bulletin, 84,* 1189–1217.

Bowers, C.A., Weaver, J.L. & Morgan, B.B. (1996). Moderating the performance effects of stressors. In J. Driskell & E. Salas (Eds.), *Stress and human performance* (pp. 163–192). Hillsdale: Erlbaum.

Bowman, M. (1997). *Individual differences in post-traumatic response: Problems with the adversity-distress connection.* Mahwah: Erlbaum.

Briggs, J. (1988). *Fire in the crucible: The alchemy of creative genius.* New York: St. Martin's Press.

Brooks, G. (1998). *A new psychotherapy for traditional men.* San-Francisco: Jossey-Bass.

Buckingham, M. & Coffman, C. (1999). *First, break all the rules: What the world's greatest managers do differently.* New York: Simon & Schuster.

Bull, S.J., Shambrook, C.J., James, W. & Brooks, J.E. (2005). Towards an understanding of mental toughness in elite English cricketers. *Journal of Applied Sport Psychology, 17,* 209–227.

Burns, S.D. (2006). Surviving hostile encounters: A veteran officer's view. *FBI Law Enforcement Bulletin,* March, pp. 10–12.

Calhoun, L.G. & Tedeschi, R.G. (1999). *Facilitating post-traumatic growth.* Mahwah, NJ: Erlbaum.

Cannon, W.B. (1914). The interrelations of emotions as suggested by recent physiological researchers. *American Journal of Psychology, 25,* 256–282.

Cannon, W.B. (1939). *The wisdom of the body.* Philadelphia: Norton.

Caplan, G. & Killilea, M. (1976). *Support systems and mutual help.* New York: Grune & Stratton.

Carlier, I.V.E. & Gersons, B.P.R. (1995). Partial PTSD: The issue of psychological scars and the occurrence of PTSD symptoms. *Journal of Nervous and Mental Disease, 183,* 107–109.

Carlier, I.V.E., Lamberts, R.D. & Gersons, B.P.R. (1997). Risk factors for post-traumatic stress symptomatology in police officers: A prospective analysis. *Journal of Nervous and Mental Disease, 185,* 498–506.

Charcot, J.M. (1887). *Lecons sur les maladies du system nerveux* Vol. 3). Paris: Progress Medical.

Chase, W.G. & Simon, H.A. (1973). Perception in chess. *Cognitive Psychology, 4,* 55–81.

Chi, M., Feltovich, P.J. & Glaser, R. (1981). Categorization and representation of physics problems by experts and novices. *Cognitive Science, 5,* 121–152.

Clary, M. (2005). War vets besieged by stress. *South Florida Sun-Sentinel,* March 28, pp. 1–2.

Cloherty, J.J. (2004). Legal defense of law enforcement officers in police shooting cases. In V. Lord (Ed.), *Suicide by cop: Inducing officers to shoot* (pp. 85–150). Flushing: Looseleaf Law Publications.

Cohen, A. (1980). "I've killed that man 10,000 times." *Police, 3,* 4.

Curran, S. (2003). Separating fact from fiction about police stress. *Behavioral Health Management, 23,* 1–2.

Cohn, P.J. (1990). Pre-performance routines in sport: Theoretical and practical applications. *The Sport Psychologist, 4,* 301–312.

Collins, J. (2001). *Good to great: Why some companies make the leap...and others don't.* New York: Harper Collins.

Corbett, S. (2004). The permanent scars of Iraq. *New York Times Magazine,* February 15, pp. 34–41, 56–61.

Csikszentmihalyi, M. (1990). *Flow: The psychology of optimal experience.* New York: Harper & Row.

Cummings, J.P. (1996). Police stress and the suicide link. *The Police Chief,* October, pp. 85–96.

Curran, S. (2003). Separating fact from fiction about police stress. *Behavioral Health Management, 23,* 1–2.

Davis, G.C. & Breslau, N. (1994). Post-traumatic stress disorder in victims of civilian and criminal violence. *Psychiatric Clinics of North America, 17,* 289–299.

Davis, K.R. (2005). Building search: Tactics for the patrol officer. *Law and Order,* November, pp. 51–52.

DeAngelis, T. (1995). Firefighters's PTSD at dangerous levels. *APA Monitor,* February, pp. 36–37.

Decety, J. (1996). The neurophysiological basis of motor imagery. *Behavioral Brain Research, 77,* 45–52.

De Groot, A. (1965). *Thought and choice in chess.* The Hague: Mouton.

De Groot, A. (1966). Perception and memory versus thought: Some old ideas and recent findings. In B. Kleinmuntz (Ed.), *Problem solving.* New York: Wiley.

Dienstbier, R. A. (1989). Arousal and physiological toughness: Implications for mental and physical health. *Psychological Review,* 96:84–100.

Doss, W. (2006). Exercising emotional control. *Police,* March, pp. 68–73.

Doss, W. (2007). *Condition to win: Dynamic techniques for performance oriented mental conditioning.* Flushing, NY: Looseleaf Law Publications, Inc.

Dunning, C. (1999). Postintervention strategies to reduce police trauma: A paradigm shift. In J.M. Violanti & D. Paton (Eds.), *Police trauma: Psychological aftermath of civilian combat* (pp. 269–289). Springfield: Charles C. Thomas.

Duran, P.L. (1999). *Developing the survival attitude: A guide for the new officer.* Flushing, NY: Looseleaf Law Press.

Durham, T.W., McCammon, S.L. & Allison, E.J. (1985). The psychological impact of disaster on rescue personnel. *Annals of Emergency Medicine, 14,* 664–668.

Dyregrov, A. (1989). Caring for helpers in disaster situations: Psychological debriefing. *Disaster Management, 2,* 25–30.

Dyregrov, A. (1997). The process in psychological debriefing. *Journal of Traumatic Stress, 10,* 589–605.

Ericsson, K.A., Krampe, R.T. & Tesch-Romer, C. (1993). The role of deliberate practice in the acquisition of expert performance. *Psychological Review, 100,* 363–406.

Evans, R.W. (1992). The post-concussion syndrome and the sequelae of mild head injury. *Neurologic Clinics, 10,* 815–847.

Everly, G.S., Flannery, R.B. & Mitchell, J.T. (2000). Critical incident stress management: A review of the literature. *Aggression and Violent Behavior, 5,* 23–40.

Everly, G.S. & Mitchell, J.T. (1997). *Critical incident stress management (CISM): A new era and standard of care in crisis intervention.* Ellicott City: Chevron.

Everstine, D.S. & Everstine, L. (1993). *The trauma response: Treatment for emotional injury.* New York: Norton.

Ferenczi, S., Abraham, K. & Simmel, E. (1921). *Psychoanalysis and the war neuroses.* Vienna: International Psycho-Analysis Press.

Flannery, R.B., Fulton, P. & Tausch, J. (1991). A program to help staff cope with psychological sequelae of assaults by patients. *Hospital and Community Psychiatry, 42,* 935–938.

Flin, R. (1996). *Sitting in the hot seat: Leaders and teams for effective critical incident management.* New York: Wiley.

Frazier, F. & Wilson, R.M. (1918). The sympathetic nervous system and the "irritable heart of soldiers." *British Medical Journal, 2,* 27–29.

Freud, S. (1920). Beyond the pleasure principle. In J. Strachey (Ed. & Transl.), *The standard edition of the complete psychological works of Sigmund Freud* (Vol. XVIII, pp. 7–64). New York: Norton.

Fullerton, C.S., McCarroll, J.E., Ursano, R.J. & Wright, K.M. (1992). Psychological responses of rescue workers: Firefighters and trauma. *American Journal of Orthopsychiatry, 62,* 371–378.

Gal-Or, Y, Tenenbaum, G., Furst, D. & Shertzer, M. (1985). Effect of self-control and anxiety on training performance in young and novice parachuters. *Perceptual and Motor Skills, 60,* 743–746.

Galovski, T. & Lyons, J.A. (2004). Psychological sequelae of combat violence: A review of the impact of PTSD on the veteran's family, and possible interventions. *Aggression and Violent Behavior, 9,* 477–501.

Gardner, R.W., Holzman, P.S., Klein, G.S., Linton, H.B. & Spence, D.P. (1959). Cognitive control: A study of individual consistencies in cognitive behavior. *Psychological Issues, 1,* 1–185.

Garmezy, N. (1991). Resilience and vulnerability to adverse developmental outcomes associated with poverty. *American Behavioral Scientist, 34,* 416–430.

Garner, G.W. (1995). *Common sense police supervision: A how-to manual for the first-line supervisor* (2nd ed.). Springfield: Charles C Thomas.

Garner, G.W. (2005). *Surviving the street: Officer safety and survival techniques.* Springfield, IL: Charles C Thomas.

Geller, W.A. (1982). Deadly force: What we know. *Journal of Police Science and Administration, 10,* 151–177.

Geller, W.A. & Toch, H. (1996). Understanding and controlling police abuse of force. In W.A. Geller & H. Toch (Eds.), *Police violence: Understanding and controlling police abuse of force* (pp. 292–328). New Haven: Yale University Press.

Gentz, D. (1991). The psychological impact of critical incidents on police officers. In J. Reese, J. Horn & C. Dunning (Eds.), *Critical incidents in policing* (pp. 119–121). Washington DC: US Government Printing Office.

Gigerenzer, G., Hoffrage, U. & Kleinbolting, H. (1991). Probabilistic mental models: A Brunswikian theory of confidence. *Psychological Review, 98,* 506–528.

Gilliland, B.E. & James, R.K. (1993). *Crisis intervention strategies* (2nd ed.). Pacific Grove: Brooks/Cole.

Goldberg, A.S. (1998). *Sports slump-busting: 10 steps to mental toughness and peak performance.* Champaign, IL: Human Kinetics.

Gore, J., Banks, A., Millward, L. & Kyriakidou, O. (2006). Naturalistic decision making and organizations: Reviewing pragmatic science. *Organization Studies, 27,* 925–942.

Gould, D., Hodge, K., Peterson, K. & Petlichkoff, L. (1987). Psychological foundations of coaching: Similarities and differences among intercollegiate wrestling coaches. *The Sport Psychologist, 1,* 293–308.

Griffith, J. (1989). The army's new unit personnel replacement and its relationship to unit cohesion and social support. *Military Psychology, 1,* 17–34.

Gudjonsson, G.H. & Adlam, K.R. (1985). Occupational stressors among British police officers. *Police Journal, 58,* 73–80.

Hanin, Y. (2000). Individual zones of optimal functioning (IZOF) model: Emotion-performance relationships in sport. In Y. Hanin (Ed.), *Emotions in sport* (pp. 65–89). Champaign, IL: Human Kinetics.

Hardy, L., Jones, G. & Gould, D. (1996). *Understanding psychological preparation for sport: Theory and practice of elite performers.* New York: Wiley.

Haughton, B. (2005). 10 things for patrol . . . when SWAT is on the way. *Law and Order,* November, pp. 40–48.

Hays, K.F. & Brown, C.H. (2004). *You're on! Consulting for peak performance.* Washington DC: American Psychological Association.

Hedlund, J., Forsythe, G.B., Horvath, J.A., Williams, W.M., Snook, S. & Sternberg, R.J. (2003). Identifying and assessing tacit knowledge: Understanding the practical intelligence of military leaders. *Leadership Quarterly, 14,* 117–140.

Henry, V.E. (2004). *Death work: Police, trauma, and the psychology of survival.* New York: Oxford University Press.

Higgins, G.O. (1994). *Resilient adults: Overcoming a cruel past.* San Francisco: Jossey-Bass.

Hogan, J. & Lesser, M. (1996). Selection of personnel for hazardous performance. In J. Driskell & E. Salas (Eds.), *Stress and human performance* (pp. 195–222). Hillsdale: Erlbaum.

Honig, A.L. & Roland, J.E. (1998). Shots fired: Officer involved. *The Police Chief,* October, pp. 65–70.

Honig, A.L. & Sultan, E. (2004). Reactions and resilience under fire: What an officer can expect. *The Police Chief,* December, pp. 54–60.

Horn, J.M. (1991). Critical incidents for law enforcement officers. In J.T. Reese, J.M. Horn & C. Dunning (Eds.), *Critical incidents in policing* (rev. ed., pp. 143–148). Washington DC: Federal Bureau of Investigation.

Horowitz, M.J. (1986). *Stress response syndromes* (2nd ed.). New York: Jason Aronson.

Hulse, L.M. & Memon, A. (2006). Fatal impact: The effects of emotional arousal and weapon presence on police officers' memories for a simulated crime. *Legal and Criminological Psychology, 11,* 313–325.

Huppert, J.D. & Baker-Morrisette, S.L. (2003). Beyond the manual: The insider's guide to panic control treatment. *Cognitive and Behavioral Practice, 10,* 2–13.

Ievleva, L. & Orlick, T. (1991). Mental links to enhanced healing: An exploratory study. *The Sport Psychologist, 5,* 25–40.

International Association of Chiefs of Police (2004). *Officer-involved shooting guidelines.* Los Angeles: IACP.

Jackson, S. & Csikszentmihalyi, M. (1999). *Flow in sports.* Champaign, IL: Human Kinetics.

Janik, J. (1991). What value are cognitive defenses in critical incident stress? In J. Reese, J. Horn & C. Dunning (Eds.), *Critical incidents in policing* (pp. 149–158). Washington DC: US Government Printing Office.

Janis, I. & Mann, L. (1977). *Decision making.* New York: Free Press.

Janoff-Bulman, R. (1992). *Shattered assumptions.* New York: Free Press.

Jeannerod, M. (1995). Mental imagery in the motor context. *Neuropsychologia, 33,* 1419–1432.

Johnson, J.H. & Cannon-Bowers, J.A. (1996). Training for stress exposure. In J. Driskell & E. Salas (Eds.), *Stress and human performance* (pp. 223–256). Hillsdale: Erlbaum.

Johnson, P.E., Duran, A.S., Hassebrock, F., Moller, J., Prietula, M., Feltovich, P.J. & Swanson, D.B. (1981). Expertise and error in diagnostic reasoning. *Cognitive Science, 5,* 235–283.

Johnson, P.E., Johnson, M.G. & Little, R.K. (1984). Expertise in trial advocacy: Some considerations for inquiry into its nature and development. *Campbell Law Review, 7,* 119–143.

Jones, J.G., Hanton, S. & Connaughton, D. (2002). What is this thing called mental toughness? An investigation of elite performers. *Journal of Applied Sport Psychology, 14,* 205–218.

Kanki, B.G. (1996). Stress and aircrew performance: A team-level perspective. In J. Driskell & E. Salas (Eds.), *Stress and human performance* (pp. 126–162). Hillsdale: Erlbaum.

Kabat-Zinn, J. (1994). *Wherever you go, there you are: Mindfulness meditation in everyday life.* New York: Hyperion.

Kabat-Zinn, J. (2003). Mindfulness-based interventions in context: Past, present, and future. *Clinical Psychology: Science and Practice, 10,* 144–156.

Kardiner, A. (1941). *The traumatic neuroses of war.* Washington DC: National Research Council.

Karlsson, I. & Christianson, S.A. (2003). The phenomenology of traumatic experiences in police work. *Policing: An International Journal of Police Strategies and Management, 26,* 419–438.

Kavanaugh, E.L. (2006). A cognitive model of firearms policing. *Journal of Police and Criminal Psychology, 21,* 25–36.

Keinan, G. & Friedland, N. (1996). Training effective performance under stress: Queries, dilemmas, and possible solutions. In J. Driskell & E. Salas (Eds.), *stress and human performance* (pp. 257–277). Mahwah: Erlbaum.

Kirschman, E.F. (1997). *I love a cop: What police families need to know.* New York: Guilford.

Klein, G.A. (1989). Recognition-primed decisions. In W. Rouse (Ed.), *Advances in man-machine systems research* (Vol. 5, pp. 47–92). Greenwich, CT: JAI Press.

Klein, G.A. (1993). A recognition-primed decision (RPD) model of rapid decision making. In G. Klein, J. Orasanu, R. Calderwood & C. Zsambok (Eds.), *Decision making in action* (pp. 79–103). New York: Ablex.

Klein, G.A. (1996). The effect of acute stressors on decision making. In J. Driskell & E. Salas (Eds.), *Stress and human performance* (pp. 49–88). Hillsdale: Erlbaum.

Klein, G.A. (1998). *Sources of power: How people make decisions.* Cambridge: MIT Press.

Klein, G.S. (1954). Need and regulation. In M.R. Jones (Ed.), *Nebraska symposium on motivation.* Lincoln: University of Nebraska Press.

Kobassa, S.C.O., Maddi, S. & Cahn, S. (1982). Hardiness and health: A prospective study. *Journal of Personality and Social Psychology, 42,* 168–177.

Lane, J.F. (1980). Improving athletic performance through visuo-motor behavior rehearsal. In R.M. Suinn (Ed.), *Psychology in sport: Methods and applications.* Minneapolis: Burgess.

Lazarus, R.S. & Folkman, S. (1984). *Stress, appraisal, and coping.* New York: McGraw-Hill.

Leigh, T.W. (1987). Cognitive selling scripts and sales training. *Journal of Personal Selling and Sales Management, 7,* 39–48.

Leigh, T.W. & McGraw, P.F. (1989). Mapping the procedural knowledge of industrial sales personnel: A script-theoretic investigation. *Journal of Marketing, 53,* 16–34.

Leinhardt, G. & Greeno, J.G. (1986). The cognitive skill of teaching. *Journal of Educational Psychology, 78,* 75–95.

Leong, S.M., Busch, P.S. & John, D.R. (1989). Knowledge bases and salesperson effectiveness: A script-theoretic analysis. *Journal of Marketing Research, 26,* 164–178.

Locke, E.A., Frederick, E., Lee, C. & Bubko, P. (1984). Effect of self-efficacy goals and task strategy on task performance. *Journal of Applied Psychology, 64,* 241–251.

Loehr, J.E. (1995). *The new toughness training for sports.* New York: Penguin.

Loftus, E.F., Greene, E.L. & Doyle, J.M. (1989). The psychology of eye-witness testimony. In D.C. Raskin (Ed.), *Psychological Methods in Criminal Investigations and Evidence* (pp. 3–46). New York: Springer.

Loftus, E., Loftus, G. & Messo, J. (1987). Some facts about "weapon focus." *Law and Human Behavior, 11,* 55–62.

Luthar, S.S., Cicchetti, D. & Becker, B. (2000). The construct of resilience: A critical evaluation and guidelines for future work. *Child Development, 71,* 543–562.

Marra, T. (2005). *Dialectical behavior therapy in private practice: A practical and comprehensive guide.* Oakland, CA: New Harbinger.

Maslow, A.H. (1968). *Toward a psychology of being* (2nd ed.). Princeton: VanNostrand.

Masten. A.S. & Coatsworth, J.D. (1998). The development of competence in favorable and unfavorable environments: Lessons from research on successful children. *American Psychologist, 53,* 205–220.

Matsakis, A. (1994). *Post-traumatic stress disorder: A complete treatment guide.* Oakland, CA: New Harbinger.

Max, D.J. (2000). The cop and the therapist. *New York Times Magazine,* December 3, pp. 94–98.

Maynard, P.E. & Mary, E. (1982). Stress in police families: Some policy implications. *Journal of Police Science and Administration, 10,* 422–439.

McCann, I.L. & Pearlman, L.A. (1990). *Psychological trauma and the adult survivor: Theory, therapy, and transformation.* New York: Brunner/Mazel.

Matsuo, M. & Kusumi, T. (2002). Salesperson's procedural knowledge, experience, and performance: An empirical study in Japan. *European Journal of Marketing, 26,* 840–854.

Martens, R. (1987). *The coach's guide to sport psychology.* Champaign, IL: Human Kinetics.

Max, D.J. (2000). The cop and the therapist. *New York Times Magazine,* December 3, pp. 94–98.

McCann, I.L. & Pearlman, L.A. (1990). *Psychological trauma and the adult survivor: Theory, therapy, and transformation.* New York: Brunner/Mazel.

McMains. M.J. (1986a). Post-shooting trauma: Demographics of professional support. In J.T. Reese & H. Goldstein (Eds.), *Psychological services for law enforcement* (pp. 361–364). Washington DC: US Government Printing Office.

McMains. M.J. (1986b). Post-shooting trauma: Principles from combat. In J.T. Reese & H. Goldstein (Eds.), *Psychological services for law enforcement* (pp. 365–368). Washington DC: US Government Printing Office.

McMains, M.J. (1991). The management and treatment of postshooting trauma. In J.T. Horn & C. Dunning (Eds.), *Critical incidents in policing* (rev ed., pp. 191–198). Washington DC: Federal Bureau of Investigation.

McNally, R.J., Bryant, R.A. & Ehlers, A. (2003). Does early psychological intervention promote recovery from post-traumatic stress? *Psychological Science in the Public Interest, 4,* 45–79.

Mearburg, J.C. & Wilson, R.M. (1918). The effect of certain sensory stimulations on respiratory and heart rate in cases of so-called "irritable heart." *Heart, 7,* 17–22.

Meek, C.L. (1990). Evaluation and assessment of post-traumatic and other stress-related disorders. In C.L. Meek (Ed.), *Post-traumatic stress disorder: Assessment, differential diagnosis, and forensic evaluation* (pp. 9–61). Sarasota, FL: Professional Resource Exchange.

Merskey, H. (1992). Psychiatric aspects of the neurology of trauma. *Neurologic Clinics, 10,* 895–905.

Miller, L. (1988). The emotional brain. *Psychology Today,* February, pp. 34–42.

Miller, L. (1989). To beat stress, don't relax: Get tough! *Psychology Today,* December, pp. 62–63.

Miller, L. (1990). *Inner natures: Brain, self, and personality.* New York: St. Martin's Press.

Miller, L. (1991). *Freud's brain: Neuropsychodynamic foundations of psychoanalysis.* New York: Guilford.

Miller, L. (1993a). Who are the best psychotherapists? Qualities of the effective practitioner. *Psychotherapy in Private Practice, 12*(1), 1–18.

Miller, L. (1993b). *Psychotherapy of the brain-injured patient: Reclaiming the shattered self.* New York: Norton.

Miller, L. (1994a). Biofeedback and behavioral medicine: Treating the symptom, the syndrome, or the person. *Psychotherapy, 31,* 161–169.

Miller, L. (1994b). Civilian post-traumatic stress disorder: Clinical syndromes and psychotherapeutic strategies. *Psychotherapy, 31,* 655–664.

Miller, L. (1995). Tough guys: Psychotherapeutic strategies with law enforcement and emergency services personnel. *Psychotherapy, 32,* 592–600.

Miller, L. (1998a). Ego autonomy and the healthy personality: Psychodynamics, cognitive style, and clinicial applications. *Psychoanalytic Review, 85,* 423–448.

Miller, L. (1998b). Our own medicine: Traumatized psychotherapists and the stresses of doing therapy. *Psychotherapy, 35,* 137–146.

Miller, L. (1998c). Psychotherapy of crime victims: Treating the aftermath of interpersonal violence. *Psychotherapy, 35,* 336–345.

Miller, L. (1998d). *Shocks to the system: Psychotherapy of traumatic disability syndromes.* New York: Norton.

Miller, L. (1999a). Treating post-traumatic stress disorder in children and families: Basic principles and clinical applications. *American Journal of Family Therapy, 27,* 21–34.

Miller, L. (1999b). Critical incident stress debriefing: Clinical applications and new directions. *International Journal of Emergency Mental Health, 1*, 253–265.

Miller, L. (1999c). Workplace violence: Prevention, response, and recovery. *Psychotherapy, 36*, 160–169.

Miller, L. (1999d). Tough guys: Psychotherapeutic strategies with law enforcement and emergency services personnel. In L. Territo & J.D. Sewell (Eds.), *Stress Management in Law Enforcement* (pp. 317–332). Durham, NC: Carolina Academic Press.

Miller, L. (2000a). Law enforcement traumatic stress: Clinical syndromes and intervention strategies. *Trauma Response, 6*(1), 15–20.

Miller, L. (2000b). Law enforcement traumatic stress: Clinical syndromes and intervention strategies. www.aaets.org/article87.htm.

Miller, L. (2000c). Traumatized psychotherapists. In F.M. Dattilio & A. Freeman (Eds.), *Cognitive-Behavioral Strategies in Crisis Intervention* (2nd ed., pp. 429–445). New York: Guilford.

Miller, L. (2002a). Post-traumatic stress disorder in school violence: Risk management lessons from the workplace. *Neurolaw Letter, 11*, 33, 36–40.

Miller, L. (2002b). Psychological interventions for terroristic trauma: Symptoms, syndromes, and treatment strategies. *Psychotherapy, 39*, 283–296.

Miller, L. (2003a). Personalities at work: Understanding and managing human nature on the job. *Public Personnel Management, 32*, 419–433.

Miller, L. (2003b). Police personalities: Understanding and managing the problem officer. *The Police Chief*, May, pp. 53–60.

Miller, L. (2004a). Good cop—bad cop: Problem officers, law enforcement culture, and strategies for success. *Journal of Police and Criminal Psychology, 19*, 30–48.

Miller, L. (2004b). Psychotherapeutic interventions for survivors of terrorism. *American Journal of Psychotherapy, 58*, 1–16.

Miller, L. (2005a). Critical incident stress: Myths and realities. *Law and Order*, April, p. 31.

Miller, L. (2005b). Command leadership under fire. *Law and Order*, June, p. 26.

Miller, L. (2005c). Driven to drink: Police officers and alcohol. *Law and Order*, August, p. 30.

Miller, L. (2005d). Police officer suicide: Causes, prevention, and practical intervention strategies. *International Journal of Emergency Mental Health, 7*, 23–36.

Miller, L. (2005e). Hostage negotiation: Psychological principles and practices. *International Journal of Emergency Mental Health, 7*, 277–298.

Miller, L. (2006a). Practical strategies for preventing officer suicide. *Law and Order,* March, pp. 90–92.

Miller, L. (2006b). Suicide by cop: Causes, reactions, and practical intervention strategies. *International Journal of Emergency Mental Health, 8,* 165–174.

Miller, L. (2006c). Critical incident stress debriefing for law enforcement: Practical models and special applications. *International Journal of Emergency Mental Health, 8,* 189–201.

Miller, L. (2006d). *Critical incidents: Myths and realities.* www.policeone.com/writers/columnists/LaurenceMiller/articles/509571/.

Miller, L. (2006e). *The psychological fitness-for-duty evaluation: What every police officer should know.* www.edpdlaw.com/FFDMiller.pdf.

Miller, L. (2006f). *Bad cops to good cops: Constructive alternatives in police discipline. Part I.* www.policeone.com/writers/columnists/LaurenceMiller/articles/135069/.

Miller, L. (2006g). *Bad cops to good cops: Constructive alternatives in police discipline. Part II.* www.policeone.com/writers/columnists/LaurenceMiller/articles/135070/.

Miller, L. (2006h). On the spot: Testifying in court for law enforcement officers. *FBI Law Enforcement Bulletin,* October, pp. 1–6.

Miller, L. (2006i). Psychological principles and practices for superior law enforcement leadership. *The Police Chief,* October, pp. 160–168.

Miller, L. (2006j). Undercover policing: A psychological and operational guide. *Journal of Police and Criminal Psychology, 21,* 1–24.

Miller, L. (2006k). Officer-involved shooting: Reaction patterns, response protocols, and psychological intervention strategies. *International Journal of Emergency Mental Health, 8,* 239–254.

Miller, L. (2006*l*). *Practical police psychology: Stress management and crisis intervention for law enforcement.* Springfield, IL: Charles C Thomas.

Miller, L. (2007). Police families: Stresses, syndromes, and solutions. *American Journal of Family Therapy, 35,* 1–20.

Miller, L. (in press-a). Line-of-duty death: Psychological treatment of traumatic bereavement in law enforcement. *International Journal of Emergency Mental Health.*

Miller, L. (in press-b). Stress, acute stress, and post-traumatic stress. In F.M. Dattilio & A. Freeman (Eds.), *Cognitive-Behavioral Strategies in Crisis Intervention* (3rd ed.). New York: Guilford.

Miller, L. (in press-c). Stress management and crisis intervention for law enforcement and mental health professionals. In F.M. Dattilio & A. Freeman (Eds.), *Cognitive-Behavioral Strategies in Crisis Intervention* (3rd ed.). New York: Guilford.

Miller, L. (in press-d). Stress, traumatic stress, and post-traumatic stress syndromes. In L. Territo & J.D. Sewell (Eds.), *Stress Management for Law Enforcement* (2nd ed.). Durham, NC: Carolina Academic Press.

Miller, L. (in press-e). *Counseling crime victims: Practical strategies for mental health professionals.* New York: Springer.

Miller, L. (in press-f). *Criminal psychology: nature, nurture, culture.* Boston: AB Longman/Pearson.

Mitchell, J.T. (1991). Law enforcement applications for critical incident stress teams. In J.T. Reese, J.M. Horn & C. Dunning (Eds.), *Critical incidents in policing* (rev. ed., pp. 201–212). Washington DC: USGPO.

Mitchell, J.T. & Bray, G.P. (1990). *Emergency services stress: Guidelines for preserving the health and careers of emergency services personnel.* Englewood Cliffs: Prentice-Hall.

Mitchell, J.T. & Everly, G.S. (1996). *Critical incident stress debriefing: An operations manual for the preservation of traumatic stress among emergency services and disaster workers* (2nd ed.). Ellicott City: Chevron.

Mitchell, J.T. & Everly, G.S. (2003). *Critical incident stress management (CISM): Basic group crisis intervention* (3rd ed.). Ellicott City: ICISF.

Mitchell, J. & Levenson, R.L. (2006). Some thoughts on providing effective mental health critical care for police departments after line-of-duty deaths. *International Journal of Emergency Mental Health, 8,* 1–4.

Modlin, H.C. (1983). Traumatic neurosis and other injuries. *Psychiatric Clinics of North America, 6,* 661–682.

Modlin, H.C. (1990). Post-traumatic stress disorder: Differential diagnosis. In C.L. Meek (Ed.), *Post-traumatic stress disorder: Assessment, differential diagnosis, and forensic evaluation* (pp. 63–89). Sarasota: Professional Resource Exchange.

Munsey, C. (2006). Soldier support. *Monitor on Psychology,* April, pp. 36–38.

Nideffer, R. (1985). *Athletes' guide to mental training.* Champaign: Human Kinetics.

Nideffer, R. & Sharpe, R. (1978). *Attention control training: How to get control of your mind through total concentration.* New York: Wideview Books.

Nielsen, E. (1991). Traumatic incident corps: Lessons learned. In J. Reese, J. Horn & C. Dunning (Eds.), *Critical incidents in policing* (pp. 221–226). Washington DC: US Government Printing Office.

Nietzsche, F. (1969). *Twilight of the gods.* London: Penguin.

Norcross, R.H. (2003). The "modern warrior." A study in survival. *FBI Law Enforcement Bulletin,* October, pp. 20–26.

Pinizzotto, A.J., Davis, E.F. & Miller, C.E. (2004). Intuitive policing: Emotional/rational decision making in law enforcement. *FBI Law Enforcement Bulletin,* February, pp. 1–6.

Nordland, R. & Gegax, T.T. (2004). Stress at the front. *Newsweek,* January 12, pp. 34–37.

Oppenheim, H. (1890). Tatsachliches und hypthothetisches uber das wesen der hysterie. *Berlin Klinik Wschr, 27,* 553.

Orasanu, J. & Backer, P. (1996). Stress and military performance. In J. Driskell & E. Salas (Eds.), *Stress and human performance* (pp. 89–125). Hillsdale: Erlbaum.

Orasanu, J. & Connolly, T. (1993). The reinvention of decision making. In G.A. Klein, J. Oranasu, R. Calderwood & C.E. Zsambok (Eds.), *Decision making in action: Models and methods* (pp. 3–20). Norwood, NJ: Ablex.

Orlick, T. (1986). *Psyching up for sport: Mental training for athletes.* Champaign, IL: Leisure Press.

Orlick, T. (2000). *In pursuit of excellence: How to win in sport and life through mental training* (3rd ed.). Champaign: Human Kinetics.

Palmer, C.E. (1983). A note about paramedics' strategies for dealing with death and dying. *Journal of Occupational Psychology, 56,* 83–86.

Paton, D. & Smith, L. (1999). Assessment, conceptual and methodological issues in researching traumatic stress in police officers. In J.M. Violanti & D. Paton (Eds.), *Police trauma: Psychological aftermath of civilian combat* (pp. 13–24). Springfield: Charles C Thomas.

Paton, D., Smith, L., Violanti, J.M. & Eranen, L. (2000). Work-related traumatic stress: Risk, vulnerability, and resilience. In J. Violanti, D. Paton & C. Dunning (Eds.), *Post-traumatic stress intervention: Challenges, issues, and perspectives* (pp. 187–203). Springfield: Charles C. Thomas.

Peak, K.J. (2003). *Policing in America: Methods, issues, challenges* (4th ed.). Upper Saddle River, NJ: Prentice-Hall.

Peak, K.J. & Glensor, R.W. (2002). *Community policing and problem-solving: strategies and practices* (3rd ed.). Upper Saddle River: Prentice-Hall.

Pennington, N. & Hastie, R. (1993). A theory of explanation-based decision making. In G.A. Klein, J. Oranasu, R. Calderwood & C.E. Zsambok (Eds.), *Decision making in action: Models and methods* (pp. 188–201). Norwood, NJ: Ablex.

Pickel, K.L. (1998). Unusualness and threat as possible causes of "weapon focus." *Memory, 11,* 277–292.

Pickel, K.L. (1999). The influence of context on the weapon focus effect. *Law and Human Behavior, 23,* 299–311.

Pinizzotto, A.J., Davis, E.F. & Miller, C.E. (2004). Intuitive policing: Emotional/rational decision making in law enforcement. *FBI Law Enforcement Bulletin,* February, pp. 1–6.

Pizarro, J., Silver, R.C. & Prouse, J. (2006). Physical and mental health costs of traumatic experiences among Civil War veterans. *Archives of General Psychiatry, 63,* 193–200.

Privette, G. & Bundrick, C.M. (1991). Peak experience, peak performance, and flow: Personal descriptions and theoretical constructs. *Journal of Social Behavior and Personality, 6,* 169–188.

Rachman, S.J. (1983). Fear and courage among military bomb-disposal operators. *Advances in Behavior Research and Therapy, 4,* 1–87.

Ravizza, K. (1977). Peak experience in sport. *Journal of Humanistic Psychology, 17,* 35–40.

Regehr, C. (2001). Crisis debriefings for emergency responders: Reviewing the evidence. *Journal of Brief Treatments and Crisis Intervention, 1,* 87–100.

Regehr, C. & Bober, T. (2004). *In the line of fire: Trauma in the emergency services.* New York: Oxford University Press.

Reese, J.T. (1987). Coping with stress: It's your job. In J.T. Reese (Ed.), *Behavioral science in law enforcement* (pp. 75–79). Washington DC: FBI.

Reese, J.T. (1991). Justifications for mandating critical incident aftercare. In J.T. Reese, J.M. Horn & C. Dunning (Eds.), *Critical incidents in policing* (rev. ed., pp. 213–220). Washington DC: USGPO.

Rodgers, B.A. (2006). *Psychological aspects of police work: An officer's guide to street psychology.* Springfield, IL: Charles C Thomas.

Rosen, G. (1975). Nostalgia: A forgotten psychological disorder. *Psychosomatic Medicine, 5,* 342–347.

Rossmo, D.K. (2006). Criminal investigative failures: Avoiding the pitfalls. *FBI Law Enforcement Bulletin,* September, 1–8.

Rostow, C.D. & Davis, R.D. (2004). *A handbook for psychological fitness-for-duty evaluations in law enforcement.* New York: Haworth.

Rushall, B.S. (1992). *Mental skills training for sports: A manual for athletes, coaches, and sport psychologists.* Australia: Sports Science Associates.

Russell, H.E. & Beigel, A. (1990). *Understanding human behavior for effective police work* (3rd ed.). New York: Basic Books.

Rutter, M. (1987). Psychosocial resilience and protective mechanisms. *American Journal of Orthopsychiatry, 57,* 316–331.

Ruzek, J.I. (2002). Providing brief education and support for emergency response workers: An alternative to debriefing. *Military Medicine, 167,* 73.

Safer, M.A., Christianson, S.-A., Autry, M.W. & Osterlund, K. (1998). Tunnel memory for traumatic events. *Applied Cognitive Psychology, 12,* 99–117.

Salas, E., Driskell, J.E. & Hughes, S. (1996). Introduction: The study of stress and human performance. In J.E. Driskell & E. Salas (Eds.), *Stress and human performance* (pp. 1–45). Mahwah: Erlbaum.

Scanff, C.L. & Taugis, J. (2002). Stress management for police special forces. *Journal of Applied Sport Psychology, 14,* 330–343.

Schraagen, K.M. & Leijenhorst, H. (2001). Searching for evidence: Knowledge and search strategies used by forensic scientists. In E. Salas & G. Klein (Eds.), *Linking expertise and naturalistic decision making* (pp. 263–274). Mahwah: Erlbaum.

Selye, H. (1956). *The stress of life.* New York: McGraw-Hill.

Selye, H. (1973). The evolution of the stress concept. *American Scientist, 61,* 692–699.

Selye, H. (1975). *Stress without distress.* New York: Signet.

Sewell, J.D. (1983). The development of a critical life events scale for law enforcement. *Journal of Police Science and Administration, 11,* 109–116.

Shale, J.H., Shale, C.M. & Shale, J.D. (2003). Denial often key in psychological adaptation to combat situations. *Psychiatric Annals, 33,* 725–729.

Shapiro, D. (1965). *Neurotic styles.* New York: Basic Books.

Sheehan, D.C., Everly, G.S. & Langlieb, A. (2004). Current best practices: Coping with major critical incidents. *FBI Law Enforcement Bulletin,* September, pp. 1–13.

Sherman, N. (2005). *Stoic warriors: The ancient philosophy behind the military mind.* New York: Oxford University Press.

Shepherd, C.D., Gardial, S.F., Johnson, M.G. & Rentz, J.O. (2006). Cognitive insights into the highly skilled or expert salesperson. *Psychology and Marketing, 23,* 115–138.

Shipley, P. & Baranski, J.V. (2002). Police officer performance under stress: A pilot study on the effects of visuomotor behavior rehearsal. *International Journal of Stress Management, 9,* 71–80.

Silva, M.N. (1991). The delivery of mental health services to law enforcement officers. In J.T. Reese, J.M. Horn & C. Dunning (Eds.), *Critical incidents in policing* (rev. ed., pp. 335–341).

Simonton, D.K. (1994). *Greatness: Who makes history and why.* New York: Guilford.

Solomon, R.M. (1988). Mental conditioning: The utilization of fear. In J.T. Reese & J.M. Horn (Eds.), *Police psychology: Operational assistance* (pp. 391–407). Washington DC: US Government Printing Office.

Solomon, R.M. (1990). Administrative guidelines for dealing with officers involved in on-duty shooting situations. *The Police Chief,* February, p. 40.

Solomon, R.M. (1991). The dynamics of fear in critical incidents: Implications for training and treatment. In J.T. Reese, J.M. Horn & C. Dunning (Eds.), *Critical incidents in policing* (pp. 347–358). Washington DC: Federal Bureau of Investigation.

Solomon, R.M. (1995). Critical incident stress management in law enforcement. In G.S. Everly (Ed.), *Innovations in disaster and trauma psychology: Applications in emergency services and disaster response* (pp. 123–157). Ellicott City: Chevron.

Solomon, R.M. & Horn, (1986). Post-shooting traumatic reactions: A pilot study. In J.T. Reese & H. Goldstein (Eds.), *Psychological services for law enforcement* (pp. 383–393). Washington DC: US Government Printing Office.

Solomon, Z. & Benbenishty, R. (1988). The role of proximity, immediacy, and expectance in frontline treatment of combat stress reactions among Israelis in the Lebanon war. *American Journal of Psychiatry, 143,* 613–617.

Somodevilla, S.A. (1986). Post-shooting trauma: Reactive and proactive treatment. In J.T. Reese & H. Goldstein (Eds.), *Psychological services for law enforcement* (pp. 395–398). Washington DC: US Government Printing Office.

Southard, E. (1919). *Shell-shock and other neuropsychiatric problems.* Boston: Leonard.

Spaulding, D. (2005). Intuitive decision making. *Police,* March, pp. 62–64.

Staw, R., Sandelands, L. & Dutton, J. (1981). Threat rigidity effects in organizational behavior: A multi-level analysis. *Administrative Science Quarterly, 26,* 501–524.

Steblay, N.M. (1992). A meta-analytic review of the weapon focus effect. *Law and Human Behavior, 16,* 413–424.

Sternberg, R.J. (Ed.), *Why smart people can be so stupid.* New Haven, CT: Yale University Press.

Stratton, J.G. (1984). *Police passages.* Manhattan Beach: Glennon Publishing Co.

Stratton, J.G. (1986). Worker's Compensation, disability, and retirement: The police. In J.T. Reese & H.A. Goldstein (Eds.), *Psychological services for law enforcement* (pp. 527–531). Washington DC: USGPO.

Stuhlmiller, C. & Dunning, C. (2000). Challenging the mainstream: From pathogenic to salutogenic models of post-trauma intervention. In J. Violanti, D. Paton & C. Dunning (Eds.), *Post-traumatic stress intervention: Challenges, issues, and perspectives* (pp. 10–42). Springfield: Charles C Thomas.

Suinn, R. (1972). Removing emotional obstacles to learning and performance by visuo-motor behavior rehearsal. *Behavioral Therapy, 31,* 308–310.

Suinn, R. (1984). Visual motor behavior rehearsal: The basic technique. *Scandinavian Journal of Behavior Therapy, 13,* 131–142.

Suinn, R. (1985). Imagery rehearsal applications to performance enhancement. *The Behavior Therapist, 8,* 155–159.

Sujan, H., Sujan, M. & Bettman, J.R. (1988). Knowledge structure differences between more effective and less effective salespeople. *Journal of Marketing Research, 25,* 81–86.

Szymanski, D.M. (1988). Determinants of selling effectiveness; The importance of declarative knowledge to the personal selling concept. *Journal of Marketing, 52,* 64–77.

Taylor, S.E. & Brown, J.D. (1988). Illusion and well-being: A social psychological perspective on mental health. *Psychological Bulletin, 103,* 193–210.

Taylor, S.E., Wood, J.V. & Lechtman, R.R. (1983). It could be worse: Selective evaluation as a response to victimization. *Journal of Social Issues, 39,* 19–40.

Tedeschi, R.G. & Calhoun, L.G. (1995). *Trauma and transformation: Growing in the aftermath of suffering.* Thousand Oaks, CA: Sage.

Tedeschi, R.G. & Calhoun, L.G. (2004). Post-traumatic growth: Conceptual foundations and empirical evidence. *Psychological Inquiry, 15,* 1–18.

Tedeschi, R.G. & Kilmer, R.P. (2005). Assessing strengths, resilience, and growth to guide clinical interventions. *Professional Psychology: Research and Practice, 36,* 230–237.

Thelwell, R.C. & Greenlees, I.A. (2001). The effects of a mental skills training package on gymnasium triathlon performance. *The Sport Psychologist, 15,* 127–141.

Thelwell, R.C. & Greenlees, I.A. (2003). Developing competitive endurance performance using mental skills training. *The Sport Psychologist, 17,* 318–337.

Thelwell, R.C. & Maynard, I.W. (2003). The effects of a mental skills package on repeatable good performance in cricketers. *Psychology of Sport and Exercise, 4,* 377–396.

Thelwell, R.C., Greenlees, I.A. & Weston, N.J.V. (2006). Using psychological skills training to develop soccer performance. *Journal of Applied Sport Psychology, 18,* 254–270.

Thelwell, R.C., Weston, N. & Greenlees, I. (2005). Defining and understanding mental toughness within soccer. *Journal of Applied Sport Psychology, 17,* 326–332.

Thibault, E.A., Lynch, L.M., McBride, R.B. & McBride, B.R. (2004). *Proactive police management.* Upper Saddle River: Prentice-Hall.

Toch, H. (2002). *Stress in policing.* Washington DC: American Psychological Association.

Toch, H. & Grant, J.D. (2005). *Police as problem solvers: How frontline workers can promote organizational and community change* (2nd ed.). Washington DC: American Psychological Association.

Trimble, M.R. (1981). *Post-traumatic neurosis: From railway spine to whiplash.* New York: Wiley.

Tyre, P. (2004). Battling the effects of war. *Newsweek,* December 6, pp. 68–70.

Tziner, A. & Vardi, Y. (1982). Effects of command style and group cohesiveness on the performance effectiveness of self-selected tank crews. *Journal of Applied Psychology, 67,* 769–775

Van Raalte, J.L. & Brewer, B.W. (Eds.). (2002). *Exploring sport and exercise psychology* (2nd ed.). Washington DC: American Psychological Association.

Vernacchia, R., McGuire, R. & Cook, D. (1996). *Coaching mental excellence: It does matter whether you win or lose.* Portola Valley: Warde.

Violanti, J.M. (1999). Death on duty: Police survivor trauma. In J.M. Violanti & D. Paton (Eds.), *Police trauma: Psychological aftermath of civilian combat* (pp. 139–158). Springfield: Charles C Thomas.

Violanti, J.M. (2000). Scripting trauma: The impact of pathogenic intervention. In J. Violanti, D. Paton & C. Dunning (Eds.), *Post-traumatic stress intervention: Challenges, issues, and perspectives* (pp. 153–165). Springfield: Charles C Thomas.

Violanti, J.M. & Aron, F. (1995). Police stressors: Variations in perception among police personnel. *Journal of Criminal Justice, 23,* 287–294.

Wadman, R.C. & Ziman, S.M. (1993). Courtesy and police authority. *FBI Law Enforcement Bulletin,* February, pp. 23–26.

Weinberg, R. & Gould, D. (1995). *Foundations of sport and exercise psychology.* Champaign: Human Kinetics.

Weiner, H. (1977). *Psychobiology and human disease.* New York: Elsevier.

Weiner, H. (1992). *Perturbing the organism: The biology of stressful experience.* Chicago: University of Chicago Press.

Werner, E.E. & Smith, R.S. (1992). *Overcoming the odds: High risk children from birth to adulthood.* Ithaca, NY: Cornell University Press.

Wester, S.R. & Lyubelsky, J. (2005). Supporting the thin blue line: Gender-sensitive therapy with male police officers. *Professional Psychology: Research and Practice, 36,* 51–58.

Wickens, C.D. (1996). Designing for stress. In J. Driskell & E. Salas (Eds.), *Stress and human performance* (pp. 279–295). Mahwah: Erlbaum.

Williams, J. & Krane, V. (1997). Psychological characteristics of peak performance. In J. Williams (Ed.), *Applied sport psychology: Personal growth to peak performance* (pp. 137–147). Mountain View: Mayfield.

Williams. M.B. (1999). Impact of duty-related death on officers' children: Concepts of death, trauma reactions, and treatment. In J.M. Violanti & D. Paton (Eds.), *Police trauma: Psychological aftermath of civilian combat* (pp. 159–174). Springfield: Charles C Thomas.

Williams, T. (1991). Counseling disabled law enforcement officers. In J.T. Reese, J.M. Horn & C. Dunning (Eds.), *Critical incidents in policing* (pp. 377–386). Washington DC: Federal Bureau of Investigation.

Wilson, J.P. (1994). The historical evolution of PTSD diagnostic criteria: From Freud to DSM-IV. *Journal of Traumatic Stress, 7,* 681–698.

Wittrup, R.G. (1986). Police shooting—An opportunity for growth or loss of self. In J.T. Reese & H. Goldstein (Eds.), *Psychological services for law enforcement* (pp. 405–408). Washington DC: US Government Printing Office.

Yalom, I.D. (1980). *Existential psychotherapy.* New York: Basic Books.

Zuckerman, M. (1991). *Psychobiology of personality.* New York: Cambridge University Press.

INDEX

line-of-duty death debriefing
(LODD), 117–118
purpose, scope of, 119–120
salutogenic debriefing, 119
see also individual counseling
models
decision-making
and mental conditioning
(toughness), 35–37
deep breathing technique
for pre-incident mental toughness
training, 53–54
defeat, psychology of
and surviving life and death
encounters, 88
defense mechanisms
individual counseling and,
130–132
defusing
OIS on-scene psychological
intervention, 171
déjà vu
officer-involved shootings (OIS)
and, 166
denial
defense mechanism, individual
counseling and, 131
posttraumatic stress syndrome
(PTSD) symptom, 102
depression
officer-involved shootings (OIS)
and, 167
*Diagnostic and Statistical Manual of
Mental Disorders* (APA, 1980,
2000), 8
diaphragmatic breathing
for pre-incident mental toughness
training, 53–54
direction of focus
external focus, 61
disability syndromes
traumatic disability syndrome, 101
see also posttraumatic stress
syndrome (PTSD)
displacement/projection
defense mechanism, individual
counseling and, 131
disqualifying the positive

cognitive restructuring of, 79–80
dopamine
arousal control and, 51
duration
of attention, concentration, 61–62

E
epidemiology model
of crisis prevention, 13–14
error analysis and correction
imagery training for pre-incident
mental toughness training, 69
existential toughness
individual counseling and, 134–135
expertise
adaptive expertise, psychological
survival training for pre-
incident mental toughness
training, 94
and mental conditioning
(toughness), 29–37
external focus
direction of focus, 61
extreme stress
handling
see pre-incident mental
toughness training

F
fatigue
officer-involved shootings (OIS)
and, 166
fearfulness
officer-involved shootings (OIS)
and, 167
flashbacks
officer-involved shootings (OIS)
and, 166
flexibility
of attention, concentration, 62
flow experience
and mental conditioning
(toughness), 37–39
focus
attentional focus
for increasing arousal for pre-
incident mental toughness
training, 49

Notes

Other Titles of Interest
from Looseleaf Law Publications, Inc.

Condition to Win
Dynamic Techniques for Performance-Oriented Mental Conditioning
by Wes Doss

The Verbal Judo Way of Leadership
*Empowering the **Thin Blue Line** from the Inside Up*
by Dr. George Thompson & Gregory A. Walker

The DART System: Duran Advanced Role-Play Training System
by Phil Duran

A Practical Career Guide for Criminal Justice Professionals
by Michael Carpenter and Roger Fulton

Conflict Resolution for Law Enforcement
Street-Smart Negotiating
by Kyle E. Blanchfield, Thomas A. Blanchfield, and Peter D. Ladd

Suicide By Cop—Inducing Officers to Shoot
Practical Direction for Recognition, Resolution and Recovery
by Vivian Lord

Path of the Warrior—2nd Edition
An Ethical Guide to Personal & Professional Development in the Field of Criminal Justice
by Larry F. Jetmore

Real World Search & Seizure
A Street Handbook for Law Enforcement
by Matthew J. Medina

The New Age of Police Supervision and Management
A Behavioral Concept
by Michael A. Petrillo & Daniel R. DelBagno

The Lou Savelli Pocketguides—
   Gangs Across America and Their Symbols
   Identity Theft—*Understanding and Investigation*
   Guide for the War on Terror
   Basic Crime Scene Investigation
   Graffiti
   Street Drugs Identification
   Cop Jokes
   Practical Spanish for LEOs

Crime Scene Forensics Handbooks
by Tom Martin
   Police Officer Patrol Edition
   Crime Scene Technician Edition

(800) 647-5547   www.LooseleafLaw.com